OREGON AT WORK

1859–2009

OREGON AT WORK
1859–2009

TOM FULLER & ART AYRE

OOLIGAN PRESS

Oregon at Work: 1859–2009

ISBN13: 978-1-932010-27-5

Ooligan Press
Department of English
Portland State University
P.O. Box 751, Portland, Oregon 97207
503.725.9410; fax: 503.725.3561
ooligan@pdx.edu
www.ooliganpress.pdx.edu

Library of Congress Cataloging-in-Publication Data

Fuller, Tom, 1959-
  Oregon at work : 1859-2009 / Tom Fuller & Art Ayre.
    p. cm.
  Includes index.
  ISBN 978-1-932010-27-5
  1. Labor--Oregon--History. 2. Oregon--History--1859- I. Ayre, Art. II. Title.
  HD8083.O7F85 2009
  331.09795--dc22

                        2009002193

For information contact Ooligan Press at Portland State University, Portland, Oregon.

Cover photo credits:
Dressmaking and Alteration Shop, early 1900s—courtesy Oregon State Library
An employee of Gunderson Incorporated in Portland welds parts of a railroad car—courtesy Oregon Employment Department
Workers picking hops—courtesy Oregon Historical Society
Bucking a spruce log in Tillamook County, ca late 19th century—courtesy Oregon State Library
Worker on transmission lines at Bonneville Dam—courtesy Oregon State Library

Contents

Undercutting a tree—courtesy Oregon State Library

Acknowledgments

The authors would like to acknowledge some of those without whom this book would not be possible: Laurie Warner, and Bill Fink—Director and Deputy Director of the Oregon Employment Department who provided us the time and support to bring this project to fruition. Members of the Communications and Research staff including Craig Spivey, Todd Brown, Paul Marche, Jill Read, Brooke Jackson-Winegardner, Charles B. Johnson, and Jessica Nelson. Christy Van Heukelem provided a tremendous amount of research for this project. Appreciation also goes to Lindy, Maxine, and Gloria for their assistance in reviewing the manuscript.

We would also like to thank the following organizations for their support and assistance: Sons & Daughters of the Oregon Pioneers, Salem Public Library, Oregon State Library, Mission Mill Museum (Keni Stugeon & Tracy Stroud), Sisters of the Holy Names (Sarah Cantor), Tigard Historical Society, Yamhill County Historical Society, Southern Oregon Historical Society, Polk County Historical Society, Oregon Historical Society, Crown Point Historical Society, the Confederated Tribes of the Grand Ronde, Oregon Small Woodland Owners Association, and Oregon Department of Agriculture Century Farm & Ranch Program.

This project would not have been possible without the partnership of Ooligan Press and their fine staff of editors including Ian VanWyhe, Mel Wells, Leah Sims, and Scott Parker, and this book's designer, Kelley Dodd.

Finally, we would like to thank the family members descended from Oregon pioneers who faithfully kept records, photographs, and stories safe, preserving a vital part of Oregon's history for all of us.

Preface

The Authors

This book was over one hundred and fifty years in the making, and took nearly two years to produce. Our purpose was simple: chart the evolution of something very familiar to all of us—our jobs—from the beginning of statehood until today. We sought help from those who could best help us understand how work has changed—descendants of Oregon pioneer and Native American families present when Oregon became a state. For well over a year we traveled throughout Oregon, sitting across kitchen tables from men and women who showed us treasures, carefully guarded and cared for—irreplaceable photos, journals, diaries, and artifacts—and told us equally cared for stories about the work of their ancestors.

Tom Fuller

To help put all this in context we combed through old census data, public records, research journals, articles, books, and statistics. We studied economic factors, cost of living statistics, and political, demographic, and population changes that affected how work is performed.

What emerged paints a picture of a work environment that changed from individuals primarily laboring for themselves to produce goods and services to working for someone else in order to purchase goods and services. As Oregon grew we became more dependent on one another, more specialized in the jobs we perform, and more and more influenced by economic factors beyond our borders and largely beyond our control.

Art Ayre

We hope you enjoy the many stories and photos of Oregonians at work. It was a labor of love we now share with you.

Tom Fuller & Art Ayre

Forewords

Governor Ted Kulongoski

Oregon is one of the best places on earth to live. This beautiful corner of America, with its majesty, bountiful resources, and gentle climate, has attracted many over the centuries—first native tribes, and then pioneers of many varieties. And that has been the continuous story of Oregon—new people bringing new ideas and new dreams, and building new lives for their families.

But those new lives required hard work. In farming. In mining. In forestry. And in manufacturing. Even while we were a territory, this work kept food on the table, grew the Oregon economy, attracted a steady stream of new residents, and lifted the human spirit. Then in 1859, one of the most important chapters in Oregon's long history was written. Through the grit and determination of a group of dedicated citizens, Oregon became a state. In 2009, we will mark this great milestone—150 years of statehood—in communities across Oregon by appreciating the past, celebrating the present, and imagining the future.

Oregon's past, present, and future have been, and will be, shaped by the men and women who work here. What they do with their hands and minds has allowed Oregon to prosper, and has inspired each generation to build on the accomplishments of the generations that preceded it. The workers of Oregon have made this state a model of service, innovation, productivity, and excellence.

The stories and information you will find in this book illustrate the lengths to which our citizens have gone to create a modern and diversified economy that combines traditional and new industries with the common thread of highly skilled, industrious, and proud workers.

That is why I encourage Oregonians to read and enjoy this book, which vividly details the history of work in our state. It is an excellent way to celebrate 150 years of statehood, and our great tradition of working hard to keep our economy strong and our quality of life the best in the world.

Theodore R. Kulongoski, Governor

Laurie Warner, Director of the Oregon Employment Department

Normally, we at the Oregon Employment Department focus on how to put Oregonians back to work. We help them through periods of unemployment, provide good information on what jobs are available, then match them up with employers who can use their skills. We've been doing that since the 1930s.

As director, I take great pride in the people who work hard to put others to work. But at a time when Oregon turns 150, we thought that instead of looking forward to your next best job, it might be fun for you to take a look back at all the people who have applied for or created jobs to help support themselves and their families over the course of Oregon's history.

This book is our agency's main contribution to the celebration of Oregon's anniversary. We hope you enjoy it. Happy birthday, Oregon!

Laurie Warner

Introduction

Tom Burnett—Photo taken by Tom Fuller

Philip Foster

The sharp crack of metal striking wood echoes through the cold fields. Tom Burnett stands under the awning of a barn, heaving an axe over his head, repeatedly bringing the blade down hard, and sending chunks of cedar flying. He's splitting wood to supply fuel for the woodstove in a nearby store.

Tom is the type of person who looks both back and ahead at the same time. Though he lives in the twenty-first century, Tom works like he's in the nineteenth. Using methods devised by his ancestors, Tom is in the process of restoring and preserving an important piece of Oregon history, with assistance from his sister, Joanne Broadhurst.

Nearly 150 years ago, this land where Tom chops firewood stood at the end of the Barlow Road—the final segment of the Oregon Trail and a famous alternate route for immigrants who didn't want to take the more dangerous and expensive ride down the Columbia River. The people who reached the Barlow Road had already traveled two thousand miles across rivers, deserts, mountains, and prairies—braving storms, sickness, attack, and starvation—to carve out a new life for themselves and create a state called Oregon.

Philip Foster, Tom and Joanne's great-great-grandfather, purchased this land, now called Eagle Creek, in 1847. Philip became one of the more than fifty-three thousand settlers who traversed the Oregon Trail or plied the waters of the Pacific Ocean to arrive in Oregon between 1840 and 1860. Philip turned his farm into Oregon's first destination resort, complete with a hotel of sorts, a store, a blacksmith's shop, and a restaurant. For many people on the final few miles of a harrowing journey, who arrived nearly starving with next to nothing, the Philip Foster Farm was a godsend. From here, fortified with food, shelter, and supplies, families spread out into the Willamette Valley and beyond, looking for land and a new life.

Tom and Joanne now work as volunteers to preserve what Philip and his family contributed to the settling of this state. To do this, they employ nineteenth-century construction methods and copy original furniture layouts and decorating designs to create and maintain a replica of the general store, and offer hands-on pioneer activities for thousands of guests. Visiting the Philip Foster Farm transports the visitor back to a time when technology meant creating a tool to do a job, and work meant laboring until the task was finished or it was too dark to continue.

The history of labor in Oregon is a history of Oregonians. From wrangling a thresher to turn out each year's wheat harvest to wrestling a new computer program to grind out each week's status report, work occupies, sustains, and to some extent even defines us. The equipment and the tasks may have changed over the years, but the can-do attitude of Oregonians remains. The following pages contain an exploration of how these tasks and equipment have changed—a history of how Oregonians have worked in the one hundred and fifty years Oregon has been a state.

Joanne Broadhurst—photo taken by Tom Fuller

Hauling wheat in 1890—courtesy Oregon State Library

Section One

1850–1900

Freight hauling in Union County—courtesy Oregon State Library

Settling a New State

The mid-eighteen-hundreds were a time of rapid change in the land now known as Oregon. Beginning in 1840, overland migrants arrived from the east in ox-drawn wagons, on mules, or even on foot. They reached Eastern Oregon by traversing the broad Snake River Valley. From there, they climbed over the mountain passes standing between them and the Columbia River Basin. While some decided to settle beside the river, most of these pioneers continued westward toward the eastern side of the snow-capped mountain called Wy'east by the native Chinook tribe, the Mult-nomah. (Today this peak is known as Mount Hood.) From there, they either braved the Columbia River's dangerous rapids or crossed one last mountain pass. Those who survived this last trial flooded into the Willamette River Valley, where they found a land of plentiful game, fertile soil, and abundant timber.

The settlers had reached the end of their journey, but not the end of their mission. Now was the time to carve out new lives, build new homes, live in a new land, and meet new people. These new people were not the only ones living here, however. Native Americans had been living in Oregon for generations. Relations between the settlers and the existing inhabitants, at first, were generally peaceful. Conflicts arose and dynamics underwent drastic shifts when the migrants' swelling numbers threatened Native American territorial claims and resources.

Not only were the mid-1800s a time of rapid—and sometimes tumultuous—change, but they were also a time of organization. Very little in the way of organized government existed in the Oregon Territory prior to the 1840s and '50s, as the British and the Americans had an agreement for joint occupancy of the area. On May 2, 1843, a group of settlers gathered at a trading center called Champoeg, along the Willamette River, just a couple of miles from the present city of Newberg. The purpose of the meeting was to discuss whether this new land should be a part of Canada (and thus England) or whether it should be a part of the United States.

One hundred and two farmers, trappers, laborers, and adventurers showed up for the meeting, fifty-two Canadians and fifty Americans. A farmer and trapper named Joseph Meek called for a vote. The fifty Americans voted unanimously to join the United States. Before a full count could be made, two of the Canadians (opposed to British ways) joined them, making it fifty-two to fifty for joining the States.

Meek was selected as Sheriff of the Oregon Provisional Government. In 1848, Oregon was recognized as a territory, and in 1859, sixteen years after that fateful meeting at Champoeg, Oregon was recognized as a state.

Life in the mid-1800s in the Oregon Territory was very different from life here today. Then as now, work was an integral part of life, but an average Oregonian's job in 1850 was quite different from the typical occupations of today. For example, most of the technology we take for granted and rely on every day had not yet been invented. Many jobs—whether skilled or unskilled—required significant physical labor. However, most early Oregon workers were up to the task; they had already passed a test of great physical exertion simply to get to Oregon.

Solomon H. Smith, who sided with America at the Champoeg vote— courtesy Oregon State Library

Joseph Meek—courtesy Salem Public Library

	Top Occupations in 1860		
1	Farmers	7,861	43%
2	Non-farm laborers	1,849	10%
3	Miners	1,793	10%
4	Farm laborers	1,260	7%
5	Carpenters and Joiners	768	4%
6	Merchants, Storekeepers, and Peddlers	459	2%
7	Blacksmiths	343	2%
8	Servants	312	2%
9	Teachers	206	1%
10	Clerks	198	1%
11	Wheelwrights	135	1%
12	Clergymen	125	1%
13	Teamsters	119	1%
14	Physicians	115	1%

Postcard of a young Indian boy—
courtesy Oregon State Library

Wheat harvest, late 19th century—courtesy Oregon State Library

The Homestead

Most labor in the Oregon Territory during this time period was necessary to meet the requirements of day-to-day survival. The first task of many immigrants was to find a place to live. Many people settled on homesteads in rural areas. Homesteads usually consisted of one-room log houses the settlers built themselves, typically with help from the nearest neighboring settlers.

In addition to housing, new arrivals had to find ways to feed themselves. Hunting was common because game was abundant. The land had to be cultivated as well, and it had to be prepared before it could be cultivated. Cutting down trees and either digging out or burning the roots was difficult but necessary work to clear enough land to plant crops. Most people planted a few acres of wheat and had a vegetable garden. If their cattle survived the journey to Oregon, they used them for meat or milk, and to start small herds.

It was a hard life, and often settlers had to rely on the generosity of their new neighbors—or even total strangers—if they ran out of food or other essentials. With little hard currency available, bartering was common, with wheat as the primary medium of exchange. Frequently, one person offered to perform labor for another as a form of payment.

John Bradford—Rogue River Indian
tribal member, date unknown—
courtesy Oregon Historical
Society—OrHi52886

The Original Inhabitants

Not all the workers in the state had traveled to Oregon. Many were Native Americans who had lived in Oregon all their lives.

The ancestors of these people had migrated to Oregon thousands of years before this new wave of settlers arrived.

In the 1850s, only about fifty tribes occupied the land that would become the state of Oregon. Many of the tribes were small bands of fewer than fifty people, especially in southern Oregon. There were far fewer than in previous centuries, as diseases brought by trappers, traders, and pioneers had decimated the native population in prior decades. The entire Rogue tribe could have numbered fewer than six hundred men, women, and children. Other tribes were much larger, although in point of fact, the word "tribe" is a bit of a misnomer. When white settlers came into the Oregon Territory, they found bands of Native Americans loosely associated by language group, with leadership mostly occurring at the village level.

It was easier for U.S. government officials to work with one leader for a large group of people, so the people in each language group were induced to appoint or elect chiefs to represent them. Government agents made treaties with many tribal groups, but disputes over whether those treaties were ever honored continue to this day. The result was that the government took most of the land originally occupied by the thirteen groups of language-related Native Americans and forced them to move onto reservations. This resulted in an alteration of the Native Americans' daily work that had gone on for many generations.

Warm Springs tribal women, ca 1880—courtesy Oregon Historical Society—OrHi96629

Living Off the Land

Native Americans

Most native tribes were hunter-gatherers. They did not believe in owning land, but rather in using its bountiful resources to provide for their clans. As natives were moved to reservations, the new circumstances, as well as U.S. government interference, forced them to till the soil and engage in farming, a job foreign to a people used to hunting, fishing, and gathering naturally growing edible plants.

Prior to being moved to the reservations, daily work for the Rogues consisted of gathering food and preparing shelter for their families. Women of the tribe made baskets that were so well constructed that food could be boiled in them. To do this, Rogue women would pour water into the baskets and then add stones that had been heated in the fire. As long as there was moisture in the basket, it would not leak or break.

Quinaby, labeled as chief of the Chemeketas, lived around the Salem area in the mid 1800s—courtesy Oregon Historical Society—OrHi76207

Unknown Native American tribe gathers for a group photo, unknown date—courtesy State of Oregon Archives Division

John Hudson, last known native speaker of the Kalapuya language, date unknown—courtesy Oregon Historical Society—OrHi55830

Sketch of a Kalapuyan in native dress, date unknown—courtesy Oregon Historical Society—OrHi104921

To the north, members of the Nez Perce, Shoshone, and Chinook tribes fished for salmon, cod, herring, and candlefish. While the men caught the fish, the women cleaned them. Some were roasted and eaten day by day, but a large portion of the catch had to be preserved for the cold winter ahead. Fish being preserved were first left on drying racks for several days. The catch was usually big, and the racks would be piled high with fish. The fish were later moved to a hut where they were smoked and stored.

John Hudson was a member of the tribes of the Kalapuya, once estimated to have ten thousand members. The Kalapuya occupied much of the Willamette River drainage south of the Oregon City falls. They were semi-nomadic, which meant they lived in winter homes but traveled throughout the Willamette Valley in the warmer months. John remembers when the land supplied well for his people. "Everything was good. No one labored (for wages). Only a man went hunting, he hunted all the time."

The economy of the Kalapuyans was based on the land. Contrary to the image many today have of the Native Americans as hunters who gathered the things they found as they hunted, the Kalapuyans actively shaped their environment to suit their needs. This was most apparent in their use of slash burning. Tribe members would burn dead trees, called snags, as well as grasslands. The fire would scorch grasshoppers, which the women would retrieve for food. The freshly burnt fields also left camas seeds loosened from their pods and ready to be harvested. The burned patches would grow into lush meadows that would attract elk, deer, more camas plants, tarweed, hazelnuts, and blackberries.

The men would dig pits into the ground to capture elk, place snares to capture small animals, and surround deer in narrow canyons and drive them over cliffs or into enclosures. They fished with spears, nets, and traps using canoes made from redwood or cedar.

Hudson remembers that hunters from the Santiam tribe, who lived just east of Albany, would circle around deer and shoot them with rattlesnake-venom-tipped arrows. Often the hunters would share small bits of meat with others in the tribe.

After signing treaties with the new government, the Kalapuyans moved from their lands. Instead of hunting and gathering, they were forced to plow and till the soil to grow crops in the ways traditional to the settlers coming over the Oregon Trail.

The Settlers

In 1860, the U.S. government performed a census of the population in the new state of Oregon. More than eighteen thousand people had occupations listed in that census. Of these, 7,861 (43 percent) of them were farmers and another 1,260 (7 percent) were farm laborers—that makes half of the employed population.

Most people making their home in Oregon had to have wide-ranging abilities. They had to be able to construct buildings; make or repair tools; plant, tend, harvest, and process food; and they had to be able to do most of these things by themselves. The biggest asset an Oregon pioneer possessed was the willingness to work hard until the job was done. Our first profiled worker, Wilson Carl, exemplified this spirit of hard work.

Carpenter and Farmer—Wilson Carl

Wilson Carl arrived alone in Oregon in 1853 with only "an extremely poor suit of clothes, which he wore, and his willing hands." Those willing hands had been trained in shoemaking and carpentry. It is with the latter skill that Wilson Carl began a career.

In 1855, Wilson moved to Oregon's Yamhill County, to a town called Amity. There, Wilson built a house for Solomon Allen. After moving to nearby McMinnville, he helped construct two wings of the Baptist College (now Linfield College). Not much is known about the project, except that each wing was seventy-two feet long.

Wilson was one of 761 carpenters in Oregon. A carpenter's work was very different in the mid-1850s from what it is today. A carpenter probably earned around $1.25 to $1.50 per day. Most everything had to be fabricated by hand, including doors, window casings, moldings, and stairs. Tools of the trade included a froe and mallet to cut out shingles, various planes to smooth and shape boards, hammers, chisels, boring tools, and, of course, saws. The work was slow, but the carpenter took great pride in his craft.

Wilson Carl—courtesy Warner family

1850–1899 Average Costs of Consumer Goods

Boraxine Detergent
$.10

Button Boat Shoes
$.60

Colgate Harness Soap
$.35

Demorest's Illustrated Monthly
Magazine—per year
$3.00

Flour—100 pounds
$10.00

Potatoes—per Bushel
$3.25–$4.00

Butter—1 pound
$1.00–$1.25

Wheat—1 bushel
$.75–$1.00

Peas—1 bushel
$1.00

Molasses
$.50

Candles—per pound
$.75

Bacon—per pound
$.25

Coffee—per pound
$.20

Piano
$180.00

Standard Shirt
$1.50

Chemawa Indian carpenter shop—courtesy Oregon State Library

Carpenters of the day spent many hours creating individual pieces, such as window casings, which had to be planed out of rough timber, joined together, and then installed. Just to give you an idea how slowly things could go, a carpenter might take a month to prepare the lumber and shingles, a month to make the windows, several weeks to prepare the foundation, a month or two to frame the house, a week each for siding, roofing, and flooring, a couple of days to install a staircase, a month and a half to put in windows and door casings, and another week for finish work inside. Building a fifteen- by twenty-five–foot, two-story house could begin in January and still might not be done by August, even if he had another person to help.

One thing we do know is that Wilson Carl put his tools to good use and was a hard worker. One person who knew him said, "He was always a busy man, working from early morning until late at night, and through his industry and capable management of his affairs he won a position among the prosperous residents of Yamhill County."

Buying A Farm

Wilson did well enough financially to purchase 256 acres of land, which he eventually increased to 575 acres. The land sits about seven miles north of McMinnville. One person described it "as choice agricultural land as is to be found in the country." There, gently rolling hills nudge sun-drenched acres of hay surrounded by groves of trees gently swaying in the mild Oregon weather. To the east lie thousands of acres of choice farmland. To the west sits the Oregon Coast

Range. Wilson took advantage of the rich soil of his farm and raised wheat and livestock, and continued to work as a carpenter when the need arose.

His diaries read like a combination of to-do list and weather report. He talks about working on the roads in the area, or framing, sheeting and shingling sheds and barns, then follows his discussion of this work with the weather of the day—an important thing for a farmer or carpenter to keep track of.

As a carpenter, Wilson also mentions his tools frequently. In February 1870, Wilson's journal includes, "arranged my tools in the wood house," and, "fixing up tools." He also talks about traveling to McMinnville to purchase cherry trees and of "pruning sprouted and trimmed some apple trees [*sic*]." He also filled books with lists of the prices he paid for things. They included a subscription to the *Oregonian* newspaper in 1873 for $3.00, fifteen bushels of coal for $1.88, three pounds of nails for $0.30, and four sacks of flour for $5.00.

Yamhill Stage, 1906—courtesy Yamhill County Historical Society

The Stagecoach

In those days, the stagecoach traveled near Wilson's farm on its way up into the coastal mountains. Since it was the last stop before heading into the coast range, Wilson's home soon became known as "Mountain House." Sometimes stagecoach passengers would spend the night at Mountain House. Eventually Wilson opened a post office there and was appointed postmaster.

Carlton Train Station—courtesy Yamhill County Historical Society

1880s Annual Selected Consumer Spending

Food
$120.00 – $250.00

Alcohol
$3.25

Medical
$65.00

Vacations
$.50

Rent
$21.00

Heat
$35.00

The Railroad Creates a Town

Having just the post office wasn't enough for Wilson. In 1872 he went to Portland and persuaded the Oregon Central Railroad to put in a flag stop on the recently installed railroad track that went through town, so that farmers could load crops headed to markets in Portland. (Trains would only stop in flag stop stations by prearrangement or a signal.) It proved to be one of the best shipping stops on the line for local fruit growers, stock breeders, and dairy farmers to send their goods to markets in Portland. Railroad employees started calling the stop Carl's Town. This was later shortened to Carlton, and a town was born.

In 1873, Wilson spent a number of days hauling lumber with a horse team and wagon to construct a school for the Carlton community. Wilson Carl settled so deeply that even to this day his descendants live on the farm he bought in the town he founded, a town that still bears his name. See stories of Wilson's descendants on pages 67 and 129.

The Donation Land Act

For many settlers like Wilson Carl, farming was their main occupation. The Donation Land Act, passed nine years before Oregon was granted statehood, had strongly encouraged farming in Oregon. In 1850, this act granted 640 acres—an area equal to one square mile—to married men who had lived on and cultivated the land for four consecutive years. It granted 320 acres to single men under the same conditions. After 1855, the acreages available under the act decreased to 320 if married and 160 if single.

Once claimed, creating a homestead on uncultivated land was not easy. Considering the fact that women still couldn't vote, it may be surprising to learn that not all of the land claims were made by men.

Lucinda Cox

There it was again—that otherworldly sound. Lucinda's heart beat hard against her chest, and her children clung to her skirts. The sound was like a hoarse child screaming in pain somewhere in the darkness. But Lucinda knew this was no child, no human. The cougar was back, and Lucinda wondered once again why she had moved out on her own. Worse yet, she knew she must meet this beast on its terms or die of thirst if the big cat stood between her and much-needed water.

Thomas Cox—courtesy Salem, Oregon, Public Library Historic Photograph Collections

Furniture delivery wagons in front of Buren and Hamilton Furniture Store, Salem, ca 1880s—courtesy Oregon State Library

*OREGON STATESMAN—
APRIL 8, 1856*

Rise in Wheat.—There has been a considerable rise in wheat in this market during the past week. It now commands one dollar, *cash*, per bushel. A California firm is purchasing extensively—W.C. Griswold, agent.

Lucinda's journey to independence started in 1847, on the way to Oregon and a new life. She had it all then—a loving husband, Elias, three beautiful children, and her father, Thomas, to accompany her on the long trip overland. Then tragedy took her Elias when, shortly after crossing the Platte River, he became ill and died. They buried him on the trail and then ran the wagons over the grave to obscure it from animal predators. Lucinda and her band were among the first to use Barlow Road, built by Philip Foster (see Philip's story on page 58).

Salem's First Store

Once in Oregon, Lucinda helped her father start the first store in Salem, selling valuable goods they had brought with them on the Oregon Trail. Lucinda sewed and sold clothes and hats, which she made out of silk and braided wheat straw. Her straw hats were so well-made and fashionable that Lucinda earned quite a bit of money from the operation.

Having done well at the store, Lucinda eventually decided to make a land claim. Lucinda's claim, like most of the Donation Land claims, was in the Willamette Valley, while smaller numbers of claims were scattered around the sites of present-day Roseburg, Medford, and other locations. Lucinda had a cabin built on virgin land outside of Salem. She took her children, Joseph Henry, Martha Jane, and young Elvira, and moved into the cabin, protected only by a small fence.

Mrs. Martin Hazeltine on a hunting trip, ca late 1800s—courtesy Oregon Historical Society—OrHi1579

William Hunt Wilson riding his horse—
courtesy Christy Van Heukelem

Dangers of the Wild

Perhaps she didn't know about the cougars, or the wild, aggressive Spanish cattle with the long, dangerous horns that roamed about the area, before she moved. The combination made life on the claim very difficult. Just to fetch water from the spring, Lucinda and her children had to wait until the cattle had lain down for the night. But night was when the cougars roamed, screaming and growling like wounded demons. Lucinda, alone with three children, was a small woman—weighing in at barely one hundred pounds and no match for a fully grown cougar.

Lucinda conquered her fears repeatedly but, in the end, left the cabin in Salem for good. She didn't leave because of the cougars and bulls, but to marry Hiram Allen. The couple moved to Corvallis, where she concentrated on the hard work of raising eight children of her own, as well as stepchildren and grandchildren who always seemed to be underfoot. But the sounds of children were always preferable to listening to the screaming cougars at night.

Sometimes a change from a bad situation can lead to a completely new life. Here is the story of one young man who left his home in Missouri after an argument with his father and ended up as a part of Oregon history.

Laborer, Farmer, Lawmaker—William Hunt Wilson

William Hunt Wilson settled in Oregon City after meeting Dr. John McLoughlin of the Hudson's Bay Company, who gave him a job cutting brush from the streets of the young town. Dr. McLoughlin played a key role in early Oregon history after moving here from Quebec. He was the Chief Factor (manager) for the Hudson's Bay Company, which operated out of Vancouver, on the north side of the Columbia River in what is today the state of Washington. The kind-hearted Dr. McLoughlin helped many settlers and eventually became an American citizen himself.

John McLoughlin, Chief Factor (manager) Hudson's Bay Company— courtesy Oregon Historical Society—OrHi6773

Dr. McLoughlin was pleased with William's work and soon promoted him. William went from sweeping the streets to cutting saw logs, and then to working with a gang of men putting logs into the Willamette River, at a point just south of Oregon City, for the Oregon Milling Company. William wrote:

> I had tried to do my work well and to give faithful service to the good doctor, who was regarded with greatest esteem by his employees. Perhaps he noticed that I was anxious to please, he thought me trustworthy.

At any rate, he selected me to take charge of the dry house, a position of care and responsibility.

William's job in the dry house was to stoke the furnaces that seasoned (carefully dried) lumber destined to be used in the construction of a flour mill. In addition to keeping the fires burning, he had to keep them from spreading to the dryhouse itself. It's likely this project brought him into the association of Philip Foster (see page 58), who used lumber to build a mill for John McLoughlin in Oregon City around that time.

The Laborer Becomes a Farmer

Eventually William married and settled near Yoncalla in Douglas County. He filed for a Donation Land claim and became a farmer. To increase the efficiency of his farming operation, William also began hiring men to help him, thus becoming an employer. One of the men he hired caused some controversy at the time, prior to the Civil War. The controversial hire was a man of mixed race named William Eads.

This was an unsurprising act, in retrospect, because William Hunt Wilson's road to Oregon had begun with a quarrel with his father—a quarrel over the sale of a slave he considered his friend. Before coming to Oregon, William made a lifelong friend in slavery-opponent Jesse Applegate, and Eads eventually came to be considered a part of the Wilson family. (Read Eads's story on page 47.)

William and Hannah Wilson—courtesy Christy Van Heukelem

Oregon's capitol building, used in 1862—courtesy Oregon State Library

Top Occupations in Construction	
74	Lumbermen
45	Sawyers
761	Carpenters
2	Sash makers
7	Shingle makers
20	Brickmakers
36	Bricklayers
13	Stone & Marble cutters
22	Stone & Brick masons
84	Cabinetmakers
19	Plasterers
73	Painters
21	Surveyors

William Hunt Wilson as a young man—courtesy Christy Van Heukelem

John Rickard—courtesy Benton County Museum

Mr. Wilson Goes to Salem

William's friendship with the Applegate family continued as he took a new job as Umpqua County's representative after being elected to serve in the second regular session of the Oregon Legislature in 1862. Lindsay Applegate, Jesse's brother, represented Jackson County in that same session, which lasted forty days, from September 8 through October 17. Together, William and Lindsay served on the Military Affairs Committee, which Lindsay chaired.

The setting was not very auspicious; a brick commercial building overlooking Salem's commercial district served as the capitol after a fire destroyed the first building in 1855. A second, more famous fire destroyed the next capitol building in 1935. A third fire severely damaged portions of the building in 2008. For William, fires that caused physical damage were not the only fires. Political blazes raged over controversial issues as well. At a time when the country was embroiled in a civil war over slavery, the hot issue was bound to come up. And it did.

At the time, Oregon legislators were not paid for their service, which often involved morning, afternoon, and evening sessions—and even meetings on Saturdays—deciding important issues facing this fledgling state. On the first day of 1862's second session, the Oregon Senate took up the divisive issue of slavery as it considered a joint resolution in support of the Union. Yet slavery was only a secondary consideration as the senate felt, "that the paramount objective in this struggle is to save the Union and not to save or destroy slavery." William voted for the resolution, and this was not the last slavery issue he would help decide that session.

William and his colleagues were urged to pass laws designed to prevent "Negroes and Mulatoes [sic] from coming into the state." After a failed attempt to reject the bill outright, it came to a final vote. Some like-minded colleagues joined William in his views, and they were successful in defeating that bill. But another bill, which put a tax of $5.00 on all blacks, Chinese, Hawaiians, and mulattos, passed, despite William and Lindsay Applegate's attempts to block it.

After that contentious 1862 session, William never returned to state politics, although his stand against slavery and his friendship with the Applegates continued until his death in 1902.

One of William's sayings has come down through the generations: "People can swindle you out of what I put in your pockets; but they can never swindle you out of what I put in your heads."

Farmer and Laborer—John Rickard

Pig farmer John Rickard and his family faced a serious problem. In 1854, they had forsaken Indiana for the promise of free land in Oregon. After moving to Oregon, 297 acres near Monroe in Benton County were theirs, as long as they planted a crop. Restrictions in the Donation Land Act required property owners to grow crops on the land they held or risk losing it.

Having to plant a crop was the problem—he couldn't. Not yet, anyway. First, John had to wait until the weather was moderate enough for him to break up the ground and plant. He could set out tree seedlings he'd brought from Indiana, but unless he protected them, deer or his own animals might eat them. In the meantime, he had to provide for his family until the farm could produce. That meant finding work elsewhere.

Most of the time we think of the pioneers working on their farms or in their communities, sowing crops and raising dairy cows, sheep, cattle, horses, pigs, and chickens. But sometimes that just wasn't possible. John had to look everywhere for work. The closest trading post was twelve miles away in Corvallis, but there were no jobs to be found there. So John walked thirty-eight miles from his farm to Eugene in order to work splitting rails during the week. On the weekends, he walked back to Monroe, packing supplies for his family on his back.

When not making his seventy-six mile commute, John was busy carving out a life for himself and his family, splitting rails, raising pigs, or building his own home. He also built a ten-by-fourteen-foot log smokehouse where he processed bacon from the hogs he raised on the farm. He then took the ham and bacon to sell in Portland. In 1861, a flood carried off his stock and deposited it on nearby Winkle Butte, where John recovered most of it.

Teamsters

Farms were especially common near the navigable rivers, on which people, crops, supplies, livestock, and news traveled. Thus, settlements flourished on the banks of rivers. Astute businessmen created a series of ferries to cross the Willamette River. To the north flowed the mighty Columbia. Today there are fifty-five hydroelectric dams across the Columbia, but in Oregon's early days you could navigate from the Pacific Ocean all the way to Canada by boat or barge.

Joseph Latourell—courtesy Crown Point Historical Society

Teamster—"French Joe" Latourell

"French Joe" Latourell knew the Columbia River well. As a young man, he worked ferrying cattle across the river. Later he piloted a ninety-foot scow (a flat-bottomed boat), the *Alice Julia*, up and down the river between Washougal and Vancouver. In those days there were no locks (a series of man-made pools that raise and lower ships through changes in a river's elevation) to help ships navigate, so Joe had to actively avoid many of the large rocks that made traveling up- or downriver difficult. Joe transported goods, including cordwood, on his scow to Portland.

Transportation was vital and employed not only captains, drivers, and conductors, but also ship-carpenters, saddlers, and harness-makers. Before there were very many bridges, most freight had to cross a river by ferry at some point on its journey to market. This provided a great niche business for a man who originally came west to look for gold.

Teamster — Henry Harris

In 1848, John Sutter discovered gold northeast of Sacramento, California. The news spread quickly to the East Coast and to the ears of young Henry Palmer Harris. Henry came from a large family in Cayuga County, New York. A year after the discovery of gold, the twenty-one-year-old spent $75.00 on a ticket to travel by ship and mule from New York to the gold fields of California.

Henry worked a sluice box, a narrow wooden box into which he poured dirt and rocks. He would then channel a stream through the box, which would carry away the lighter materials while gold would fall to the bottom to be collected. The work was hard, and when he stopped finding gold in his prospecting claim, Henry had to sell all the gold he had just to buy food. While prospecting and living in the Sacramento Valley, Henry also ferried rice and wheat to San Francisco. He grew tired of seeing what gold did to people. Henry was sick of the "carousing and godlessness," so he sold his claim and traveled north by ship from San Francisco to Portland.

Henry had heard that the prices for goods were more reasonable in the Oregon Territory and the land was open, sparsely populated, and available for settlement. He came up the Willamette River by one of the many steamboats that plied its waters in those days.

Mary Ellen Harris, who would marry Henry a few years after she arrived in Oregon, describes his journey this way:

> Fifteen years earlier, the way to ascend the Willamette River was to hire a crew of Indians, rowing a big bateau like a scow. These stern wheel steamers, though they appeared small and had odd lines—for they had to have a draft of not more than about three feet, to get over

the shallows in the river—were a marvelous improvement. They traveled from Oregon City to Corvallis in three days and back down to Oregon City in just one day, going with the current. There were enough steamers on the river so that one could travel almost any time. A boat started upriver at least every other day.

Hauling Freight

After leaving the ship on his journey up the Willamette, Henry walked the now-famous Applegate Trail until he got to Marysville (later renamed Corvallis). He used the money he'd saved from his ventures in California to buy a team of Belgian horses and a big wagon. Henry used the team to haul lumber at $1.00 per thousand board feet, as well as wheat and oats. Hiring Henry and his team cost $5.00 to $7.00 per day. Henry worked farmer's hours, starting at daylight and not quitting until sunset.

Despite working such long hours, Henry was able to meet, court, and marry his wife. Henry and Mary Ellen met at church in Marysville. One day Henry offered to take her across a muddy street in his wagon. They married in 1862 after a two-year courtship.

On her own year-long journey to Oregon, every piece of Mary Ellen's china had broken. She often told the story of how each time Henry delivered a drayload (a small wagonload) of wheat, he would purchase a plate or a cup and saucer for her. "It was the dearest thing. Henry loved me."

After a time, Henry decided to expand his business to include ferrying loads across the Willamette. He crossed the river by boat at a site now occupied by the Van Buren and Harrison Street Bridges—main thoroughfares between Linn and Benton Counties in Corvallis. Henry transported both people and livestock on his ferry.

Opening a Sawmill

Yet Henry wasn't satisfied with hauling other people's goods. His family back in New York State had owned sawmills, so Henry decided to build one for himself, which he operated until 1871. Henry installed one of the first steam-powered circular saws in the entire Willamette Valley. Up until that time, mills used muley saws, which went up and down. With his steam-powered saw, Henry could produce nine thousand board feet of lumber a

Freight Wagon at Klamath Lake, ca late 1800s—courtesy Oregon Historical Society—OrHi36872

Pictured is Holman's Ferry, which was used to cross the Willamette River while the Willamette Bridge was under construction from 1885–86. A flatbed wagon being drawn by two horses is in the foreground. The ferry appears to be steaming toward the eastern side of the river—courtesy Salem Public Library.

day—three times the amount produced by a muley saw. He hired loggers and mill hands, and shipped lumber all over the valley to build everything from colleges to more mills.

When the Harris family moved to the exciting new city of Newport, Henry went back to hauling cargo with his team and wagon. He worked on the Yaquina Bay Lighthouse, hauling lumber and supplies from a sawmill, and moving rocks and dirt. He even used his team of Belgian horses to raise the big timbers for the lighthouse.

Cattle Ranching

Cattle were more valuable livestock than hogs in the few settlements in eastern Oregon. Dr. John McLoughlin, Chief Factor of the Hudson's Bay Company at Fort Vancouver, herded the first cattle in the Pacific Northwest. Dr. McLoughlin, guarding the business interests of his employer, was at first hesitant to sell cattle to immigrants. But once he realized just how hard life was for them, he began lending two cows to each settler. Thanks to his generosity, Oregon soon had a thriving cattle industry—a thriving industry that took a lot of labor.

The 1850s were a boom time for the Oregon Territory. Food was in demand, and the prices were high—partly because so many immigrants streamed in on wagon trains. At the end of their journey, their supplies gone, these new inhabitants needed food. A *New York Times* article reported, "The people of this place are dependent on 'the States' for the butter, the bacon, the dried fruit, and a considerable portion of the flour of daily consumption."

Earning enough to buy food at these prices proved difficult. The average laborer earned only $3.00 a day for cutting a cord of wood. Someone with a wagon and a team of horses could earn $5.00 to $8.00 a day, but with food prices so high, even that didn't go far.

Cowboys work cattle in Umatilla County in 1890—courtesy Oregon Historical Society—OrHi80808

Why was there not enough food grown in Oregon? The *New York Times* article goes on: "The holders of 'claims' in Oregon have paid little attention to agriculture ... many of them ... have not produced more than enough grain, vegetables & [corn] for their own consumption. I am told, by those who have traveled considerable in the Territory, that there is very little good farming done here." Despite the need for and the encouragement of farming, it had not yet reached the prevalence necessary to sustain Oregon's population. Of course, hundreds of new immigrants to feed didn't help the situation.

Maybe part of the problem was Oregon's famous weather—or rather, Oregon's infamous weather—noted even as far back as 1853: "The weather here is very changeable and unsettled. It is a succession of showers and sunshine—of mild and cool weather. Last week a little snow fell—just enough to wet the ground."

It's no wonder then that there were men eager to raise beef to feed the hungry farmers, miners, and settlers—arriving by the score and having exhausted most of their supplies on the way.

David Busey

Like many young men, David Busey was in for an adventure when he set out for Oregon in 1852, traveling from Iowa with the McCully Wagon Train. At eighteen or nineteen years old, David was one of probably twenty men who ran David and Asa McCully's large herd of cattle when they arrived in Harrisburg, Oregon, on August 11, 1853.

Running cattle wasn't a high-paying job for men like David. A few years after he arrived, working on a cattle drive earned $30.00 a month in wages, though if you were a cook you could make $40.00. While on a cattle drive near Prineville, in central Oregon, David wrote to his wife, Nancy, "We have stopped on Crooked River to let the cattle rest a day or two and then I intend to move them up farther and go to Beaver Creek and look at that. I have saw several men that say that is a good contry for stock. I lost some cattle, 3 or 4 head...the...heifer fell over the graid but did not kill her nor broke any bones. I got a man to try and get her up and take care of her till I came back."

Eventually David settled in Harrisburg, and obtained a 360-acre land grant. David farmed his land and later owned a cattle ranch near La Grande, in eastern Oregon. While there, he tried his hand at gold mining as well, but without much luck. In a letter to Nancy in 1862 David wrote, "We meet men every day returning...and say the mines are no count...I am going to try my luck someway and if I fail in that my horses is in good form [*sic*]."

**The Cost of Food
In the 1850s in Oregon**

Flour
$10.00–$12.00/one hundred
pounds

Potatoes
$3.25–$4.00/bushel

Butter
$1.00–$1.25/lb
(as it came from New York
by way of San Francisco)

David Busey— courtesy Ann Horten

David was part of a small minority. Only 3 percent of Oregon's official census population in 1860 lived in the roughly two-thirds of the state east of the Cascades, all of which was called Wasco County. The sparse population and harsh conditions meant only the most adventurous people, for instance a man who'd driven a herd of cattle thousands of miles across the country, settled early in eastern Oregon.

Blacksmithing

Blacksmithing was a common occupation in the mid 1800s. The 1860 census lists 343 blacksmiths in Oregon. Blacksmiths create objects by forging them out of iron or steel. Before the days of the automobile, blacksmiths kept the transportation system going by shoeing horses and creating parts for wagons and carriages. They also would fix broken farm equipment, and make cooking utensils and fireplace tools. Before iron casting became common, blacksmiths made almost all metal tools and objects used in day-to-day life.

One of the main tools of a blacksmith was a forge, a fire made extremely hot by blowing air into it through a bellows (a chamber that forces air into a small concentrated blast). The blacksmith held metal objects in the forge using tongs. Once the piece was heated red-hot, it became malleable. The smith then removed it from the forge and placed it on an anvil (a heavy slab of metal with surfaces designed

Chemawa blacksmith shop—courtesy Oregon State Library

to help the smith shape objects), where he would strike it with a hammer, shaping it into a horseshoe or part of a wheel. Blacksmiths fell off the top ten occupations list in Oregon by 1900, but still exist today, mostly as a specialty field primarily concerned with shoeing horses.

Physicians

Facing sickness was a real part of being a pioneer in Oregon, and the availability of medical care was a real problem. Doctors were often needed but not always available. Some who claimed to be doctors or healthcare professionals were nothing but quacks.

Earlier in the century, epidemics had wiped out huge numbers of the Native Americans living in Oregon. As the populations of settlers increased and transportation improved, many of these same epidemics—including scarlet fever, smallpox, measles, whooping cough, and typhoid—decimated populations of Oregon's new residents.

So along with farmers, ranchers, miners, and merchants, medical professionals also arrived in Oregon to meet the needs of a burgeoning population. They ranged from doctors with good medical training to druggist clerks who knew nothing about medicine, but were great salesmen.

In the 1870s, the streets of Portland teemed with those who claimed to sell cures for any and every disease. One doctor, William Lysander Adams, wrote this account of the abundant medical quackery:

Portrait of Thomas Van Buren Embree, 1861, physician and surgeon in Dallas, Oregon—courtesy Oregon State Library

> Go out at 8 o'clock any evening and on most any street you will find a cure for any trouble you have of either body or soul…and one poor laboring man walks up and hands over a dollar and receives an ounce bottle of magnesia, table salt, and red pepper, nicely mixed. 'Now take a pinch of that,' shouts the doctor, 'and see if it doesn't clean out your nose.' The victim obeys and sniffs, sneezes, snorts until the tears run down his cheeks and then he laughs. He proudly shoves the package into his breeches pocket, with an expression on his face that shines out through the dirt and tobacco juice, which the crowd reads as saying, 'By golly, I think that medicine ain't no humbug.'

It wasn't until 1889 that the Oregon Legislature passed the Medical Practice Law, which required physicians to present diplomas from recognized medical schools and take an examination.

William Lysander Adams was a vocal opponent of medical quackery in early Portland—courtesy Oregon Historical Society—OrHi9148

Medical students at Willamette University, ca 1895—courtesy Oregon State Library

Most doctors spent their days treating accidents, attending childbirths, and trying to diagnose and treat diseases they sometimes knew nothing about. Most doctors also carried dental forceps in their medical bags, as dentists were rare.

It was difficult to get around on muddy roads during the rainy season, but doctors with their horse-and-buggies still attended the sick. Doctors would freely prescribe blue mass, a quack remedy high in toxic mercury; quinine, a useful remedy for malaria; and an assortment of other drugs. The kitchen table often served as the operating table. One time, Dr. Albert G. Prill had to have a family move the kitchen table out of the dim kitchen and into the sunlit out-of-doors so he could see to operate. The family also moved the stove outside to sterilize his instruments. The operation succeeded; the patient survived.

Dr. F. A. Bailey was one of the best-known physicians in Washington County in the 1860s and '70s. At the beginning of his practice, methods for surgery were still crude. Chloroform was the common anesthetic. Carbolic acid served as an antiseptic. While doctors knew little about the nature of a wound or surgical infection, Dr. Bailey insisted on cleanliness—boiling instruments, washing hands, and cleansing wounds with soap and water or with kerosene. His cleanliness helped keep his patients healthy, which in turn helped his reputation.

Dr. A. G. Prill (left) shows off his bird's nest and egg collection, date unknown— courtesy Oregon Historical Society—OrHi70179

Clergy

1888–1890 Daily Wages

Some of the immigrants to Oregon were actually invited by members of Oregon's native population. In 1832, members of the Flathead and Nez Perce tribes traveled from northern Idaho and eastern Washington to St. Louis, Missouri, where they met with General William Clark.

Tribal members told Clark that trappers living on their lands had told them of a book of great spiritual power, which they called "the white man's book of heaven." They asked Clark to send them others who could bring this power to their tribes. When news of this reached the East Coast, it sparked great interest among Christian congregations, most notably the Methodists, who recruited a young man named Jason Lee to establish a mission in the Pacific Northwest. Lee arrived in Oregon in 1834 and set up a mission near the present-day city of Salem.

Many others followed, and clergyman is listed as among the top ten occupations during Oregon's first fifty years as a state.

Luke Booth

A successful and well-known minister from Missouri, Luke Booth crossed the plains in 1865 to a settlement known as Cove. The original settlers called the place Forest Cove, but had to change it because of confusion with Forest Grove, located southwest of Portland. Nestled on the upslope of the nearby Wallowa Mountains, Cove is aptly named. Lush forest gives way to the 7,400-foot Mount Fanny.

Three years before Luke arrived, Samuel Cowles and his niece Fannie had made Cove their home, using the bed of their wagon as a living room. Not only was Cove beautiful, it also had a hot springs, which provided relief for weary travelers.

Luke raised stock and tried farming, but much of the valley was a swamp in those days. Brother Luke, as many called him, helped organize the Grande Ronde Baptist Association, and founded three churches.

Abraham Garrison

Abraham Garrison settled near Salem in 1846. As with many settlers, Abraham farmed. His real vocation, however, was that of a Methodist minister. Abraham kept a diary, which he passed down to his family, detailing his travails finding land to live on and food to feed his family.

Bricklayer
$3.55

Farm Laborer
$1.49

Painter
$2.61

Plasterer
$3.50

Plumber
$2.94

Stonemason
$3.39

Carpenter
$2.56

Engineer
$2.45

Fireman
$1.43

Luke Booth—courtesy Betty Stewart

Reverend Abraham Garrison, Methodist Minister—courtesy Oregon Historical Society—OrHi78722

He wrote: "The Yamhill country settled very rapidly—after brother Enoch moved away which I think was 1850, there was not a Methodist preacher in the Yamhill valley from head to mouth for many years except myself and I remember of fully consecrating myself to the Lord on the Plains as I lay in my wagon."

Abraham was known as a circuit rider. He was one of many such early missionaries who traveled their territories preaching and tending to widely dispersed members of their flocks. Abraham described one Sunday:

> I usually kept up summer and winter from two to three and sometimes four regular Sunday appointments, it was truly a heavy burden on me to work hard all week then of a Sunday ride from three to fifteen miles and preach then home again…I call to mind a watch-night meeting that I held at the home of brother John Miller in Polk County, I preached the day previous which was Sunday at eleven o'clock, we would sing until 9 then have a short sermon and afterwards conduct the meeting as the Lord seemed to direct, by seven the house was filled to its utmost capacity and the singing was kept up with interest until about nine when I preached a short sermon from these words 'Be ye therefore ready for at such an hour as ye think not the Son of man cometh' at the close of the sermon I invited the seekers of Salvation to the alter, there was a large number came forward and I have never witnessed just such a time before or since.

Commercial Occupations in 1860	
446	Merchants
9	Storekeepers
74	Innkeepers
55	Traders
10	Cattle-dealers
5	Horse-dealers
8	Grocers
14	Druggists
30	Bakers
32	Barkeepers
18	Brewers
65	Butchers

Not all of Abraham's ministry experiences were as successful. In 1867, he wrote about a Methodist meeting held in McMinnville where a Reverend Spencer was preaching. Right in the middle of the sermon, Abraham's son-in-law Ephraim "sprang to his feet and ordered the preacher to get out of the pulpit that he could beat him preaching." Reverend Spencer talked Ephraim down, and after Abraham remembers having to work to keep Ephraim quiet until it was his turn to speak.

Abraham was the main person responsible for building the first Methodist church in Yamhill County (in Amity), and he helped beautify the Lee Missionary Cemetery in Salem. He preached his last sermon at McCabe Chapel in 1890. He died after a protracted illness, but was a preacher to the end. His last recorded words were, "Come, come Jesus, come soon."

Women at Work

By the time Oregon became a state in 1859, the U.S. census counted about fifty-two thousand people living here. Records of wage earners were not kept until 1870; at this time, the ratio of male to female workers was forty-two to one. What this statistic really means is that while women worked very hard, taking care of their households and family businesses, they seldom earned a wage for it. Between 1850 and 1900, there were a number of conflicting forces influencing a woman's ability to earn a wage for her labor.

Women were seen as newcomers to the labor force, and were expected to work for less and take the lowest-paying jobs. At the time, about 90 percent of working women were single, and they were expected to remain in the workforce temporarily—only until they married. However, many men could not earn enough to support their families, which encouraged more women to enter the paid workforce. The expansion of cities like Portland, with the accompanying opportunities for work, also encouraged more women to seek employment.

But at the same time that economic forces were encouraging women to work, cultural forces were counteracting those forces and discouraging women from becoming employed. The strongest of these factors, perhaps, was the widespread belief held by most Americans that a woman's place was in the home, raising children and caring for the family. Despite this struggle, women contributed

Anna Louise Cronise Trover, who purchased a photography studio in 1893—courtesy Oregon State Library

Jessie Stump washing clothes. The tub is resting on a wooden chair, a washboard is in the tub. She is wearing a cloth tied over her head, and reaching down past her shoulders, ca 1880—courtesy Oregon State Library

Clothing-Related Jobs in Oregon in 1860	
Wool comber/carder	4
Weaver	11
Seamstress	15
Tailor	38
Mantua-maker*	3
Shoemaker	67
Laundress	42
Hatter	5
Jeweler	7

*A mantua was a loose gown worn over a petticoat and open down the front.

Dressmaking and Alteration Shop, early 1900s—courtesy Oregon State Library

Mary Ann Royal—missionary and noted seamstress, date unknown—courtesy Oregon Historical Society—bb004220

a great deal of labor to creating and sustaining an agricultural economy. And while the idea of women working outside of the home for money grew very slowly, it did grow.

Clothing the Pioneers

In nineteenth-century Oregon there weren't large department stores filled with racks of inexpensive clothing. Clothing was often made at home; many families purchased cloth and tailored their own clothes to save money. Some also spun their own wool and wove it into cloth. Yet many people also needed their clothes and other items made, repaired, and cleaned.

Seamstress, Nurse, and Missionary—Mary Ann Royal

Being nine months pregnant, with two young children in tow, would be enough to handle for almost anyone. But Mary Ann Royal was not just anyone. At twenty-three, she was in the midst of a perilous and difficult journey across the plains to Oregon—having walked nine miles over a rough mountain trail in one day—when her water broke.

Her labor must have been mercifully short, but her wagon train left no time for her to rest after the birth of a son, Miller, named for the captain of the band of soldiers who accompanied them to Oregon. They continued on for Oregon after only one day.

Mary Ann and her husband, Reverend Thomas Fletcher, came to Oregon to work as missionaries. When they settled in the southern Oregon town of Jacksonville, they built the first church south of Salem. Mary Ann boarded the builders and sewed ducking cloth (which is similar to khaki) by hand; it was used to cover the walls and ceiling of the church.

As there were few doctors available, Mary Ann served as caretaker for many sick miners in the area. These included a man by the name of Sampooia Kong—one of the many Chinese miners in Jacksonville at the time. When Sampooia fell ill Mary Ann took care of him, and after he recovered he converted. Sampooia was most likely the first Chinese person converted to Christianity in Oregon. Not only did Mary Ann reach out to the Chinese, but she also helped the Native Americans as well. She lived for four years as a missionary among the Siletz and served as a matron to the Klamath Indian Industrial School. She had a good relationship with the tribal members, and taught them her recipes and sewing patterns. Mary Ann also taught music, botany, and painting at the Umpqua Academy in Wilbur, Oregon, while Thomas served as principal.

Salem's woolen mill and millrace, ca 1890 — courtesy Oregon State Library

Woolen Mills

In 1857, Joseph Watt opened a woolen manufacturing mill in Salem. Other mills followed, including one built by Thomas Kay. In the early- to mid-1860s, wages in the woolen mills were $2.50 to $3.00 per day. A finisher earned $2.25 a day. In 1866, one mill was a two-hundred-foot-long by fifty-four-foot-wide building three stories high. It housed four sets of cards, seven jacks, and 1,680 spindles; cards, jacks, and spindles were parts of the large machines that turned wool into cloth. Thirty-three broad and narrow looms kept the one hundred operatives busy, producing one thousand to one thousand two hundred yards of cloth daily. The combined payroll for these workers amounted to about $60,000 a year. The skilled weavers, working ten hours a day on a piecework basis, averaged $75.00 a month.

Thomas Lister Kay, builder of the Thomas Kay Woolen Mill in Salem, ca 1863 — courtesy Oregon State Library

Teaching

Most of the early schools in Oregon were started by missionary organizations. In 1849, the U.S. Congress designated two pieces of land (called "sections") from each township in Oregon for public education. The next year the Oregon Legislature set up a system of free public schools. But creating a system and donating land was not enough to attract teachers and students, nor did it pay for buildings and books.

Caroline J. Gleason, 1886–1962

Caroline Gleason, ca 1910—courtesy Holy Names Heritage Center

Miss Gleason played a very important role in the development of Oregon's 1913 minimum wage law. In 1912 she began a survey of women workers in Oregon and recorded their wages, hours, and working conditions for the Oregon Consumer's League. The results of this survey led the Oregon Legislative Assembly to establish Oregon's Industrial Welfare Commission (IWC) in the spring of 1913. Governor Oswald West appointed the commission that same spring and Miss Gleason served as secretary of the IWC from its beginning. The commission began its work in June 1913.

By the end of 1913, it issued compulsory orders regarding women's work hours and wages. They became the model for the federal Fair Labor Standards Act. In 1916, Miss Gleason became a nun with the name Sister Miriam Theresa. She earned a doctorate in economics and supervised the social sciences department at Oregon's Marylhurst College for three decades and encouraged her students to work for society's good through the Peace Corps, Volunteers In Service To America, and in schools and prisons. Upon her death, she was eulogized before Congress.

Crook County

In Crook County, the first school house stood on the Ochoco River, ten miles east of Prineville. It was built in 1868 and there were only seventeen students in that first school term. There were literally no nails in the county at that time, so the people who built the school had to make do without. They fastened the shakes (split-log

1888 Crook County School Report

Persons of school age
1,304

Pupils enrolled
640

Teachers
13 men
24 women

Average teacher salaries
per term
$43.15 men
$38.61 women

Rural schoolhouse in Clackamas County, probably in or near what is now Milwaukie. The students and teacher(s) are outside in front of the school door. The time period appears to be 1880s—courtesy Oregon State Library

Students and teachers at school in Canyon City, ca 1880—courtesy Oregon Historical Society—OrHi82089

shingles) by using things called weight poles—heavy poles of wood that spanned across the shingles and were tied to rafters at the ends. The benches had no backs, and all the furniture was homemade.

The first term of the school lasted only three months. Parents paid for the school by subscription. Each family was also responsible for buying their own schoolbooks, which caused great confusion. The nearest store was over a hundred miles away and money for books was scarce. As a result, students didn't always end up with the same texts.

Linn County

Linn County's first school was located a mile east of Brownsville. A private school taught by Reverend H. H. Spalding, it opened in the spring of 1848 for just one month, which was all that the money raised by nearby settlers would fund.

The first public school was in Pleasant Valley near Scio and was sometimes called the Gains School. It opened for only two months that first year, 1852. The schoolhouse was built of split logs called puncheons. The school's budget for the first year was $50.00. Each family had to bring a certain amount of wood to burn in the single fireplace in the one-room schoolhouse.

Teachers in Salem, ca 1890—courtesy Oregon State Library

Arthur Prideaux—local Portland historian, presumed to be the one remembering his early school days—courtesy Oregon Historical Society—bb004219

Portland

Arthur Prideaux enrolled in the first grade at the Old North School on Tenth Avenue and Davis Street in Portland. He had to walk one and a half miles to school and sit in desks that held two students at a time. When he got thirsty, Arthur would use a large dipper to get water from a pail near the rear entrance.

The students used chalk and slates rather than pencils and paper because slates were less expensive and could be re-used after a quick washing with a wet sponge. Arthur remembers afternoons "given to rhetoricals—sometimes with visitors present." These rhetoricals were really debates using treatises such as "Resolved: Lincoln was greater than Washington." Lincoln won.

The Twelve Sisters

In October 1859, twelve women of the Sisters of the Holy Names of Jesus and Mary—a fledgling Roman Catholic community from Quebec—stepped off a sternwheeler into Portland. At the request of Archbishop Francis Norbert Blanchet of the Oregon diocese, they came to bring Catholic education to the children of French-Canadian immigrants. The sisters were young—from eighteen to thirty-three years old. Few of them spoke more than a word or two of English. Most of them had never ventured beyond Quebec. After five weeks of adventurous sea travel down the East Coast, over the Isthmus of Panama, and up the West Coast, the sisters disembarked from the ship on a gray, rainy autumn day.

Founders of the Oregon mission, Portland, 1859—courtesy Holy Names Heritage Center

At that time, Oregon had been a state for eight months. Portland's population was nearly two thousand nine hundred, making it the most populous city north of San Francisco and the major port on the Willamette River. The sisters made their way through the muddy streets to their new home, a two-story unpainted frame building with two small wings located on SW Fourth Avenue between Mill and Market Streets. One of their journal entries describes the arrival: "No key is at hand and locked doors greet us on every side. But the most ingenious removes the lock and we are finally at home, if such a scene as meets our eyes can deserve that sweet name. The lowliest hovel could not have been filthier." That night the sisters bedded down on the floor with their satchels for pillows. They had no beds.

In spite of this unpromising beginning, the twelve immediately set to work preparing to open their school for girls. In early November, not three weeks after their arrival, the sisters opened their doors to the girls of the city. Known as St. Mary's Academy, this school remains the oldest operating high school in Oregon. From the very beginning, the sisters offered education to children of all faiths; their first six students included Protestant and Jewish girls as well as Catholics.

As soon as it was clear that the Portland school would succeed, other sisters were sent to Oregon, spreading across the state to found missions and open or teach in schools in Oregon City (1860), St. Paul (1861), Salem (1863), The Dalles (1864), Jacksonville (1867), Grand Ronde (1874), and Baker City (1875). St. Mary's Academy expanded to offer normal school training, which was instruction on how to be a teacher, following the "norms" for teaching. The normal school moved to Lake Oswego when the sisters' Oregon headquarters opened there in 1911. In 1930, this became Marylhurst College. Although no longer a women's college, Marylhurst University continues to operate today.

To supplement their meager earnings from school fees, the sisters offered music and art lessons. They quickly earned a reputation not only for the excellent classical education their school provided but also for the sewing, artistic, and musical skills—skills much prized in the nineteenth century by accomplished young ladies—that they taught their students.

In November 1859, the sisters were sent a young orphan girl, their first boarder, and suddenly they were operating the state's first orphanage. Over the years, many children and infants were abandoned in the sisters' garden. Those who survived often remained with the sisters as

Drawing of the first St. Mary's Academy, formerly Lownsdale House, Portland, 1859—courtesy Holy Names Heritage Center

Nun teaches classes at Sacred Heart Academy in Salem, ca 1900—courtesy Oregon State Library

students. Eventually there were so many orphans that the sisters opened an orphanage in St. Paul. In 1908, the children were moved to the newly built Christie Home in Lake Oswego. The sisters ran Christie Home until the 1960s; it remains in operation today as a mental health treatment center for children and families.

Minorities in Oregon

The First African-American Oregonians

Some accounts say the first black resident of Oregon was a former slave named York, who once belonged to William Clark and accompanied the Lewis and Clark Expedition to Oregon in 1803. Although much mystery surrounds York's later life, William Hunt Wilson most likely met one of his offspring when he and Jesse Applegate floated down the Columbia River on their final leg over the Oregon Trail in 1843.

The 1850 census reported only fifty-five people as black or mulatto in the area in and around the present boundaries of Oregon. The majority were servants, laborers, or children living with white families. Most were poor and had few resources to make a living, despite being promised freedom from slavery.

The economic and political climate in Oregon at that time was extremely unfavorable for people of African descent. The Oregon Donation Land Act prohibited a non-white from obtaining land, and the Exclusion Laws actually sought to purge blacks from the state altogether. Of course, not everyone supported these separatist views. William Hunt Wilson was one of a courageous group of settlers that not only welcomed African-Americans, but openly opposed slavery. Unfortunately, this group's position was not the popular one, and issues of race caused much tension.

There is only one recorded incident of a man thrown out of Oregon for being black. It involves Jacob Vanderpool. Jacob owned a saloon, restaurant, and boarding house in Salem, across the street from the *Oregon Statesman* newspaper. Theophilus Magruder filed a complaint against Vanderpool. At trial, Judge Thomas Nelson found Vanderpool guilty of violating the Exclusion Law, and ordered him to leave Oregon.

The 1860 census counted only 128 blacks in Oregon (they were called "free colored" in the census). They worked mostly as farmers, miners, shingle-makers, washerwomen, barbers, cooks, blacksmiths, and common laborers.

In this hostile atmosphere, African-Americans who dared to come to and stay in Oregon became pioneers in more than one way. William Eads was one such pioneer.

William Eads—courtesy Douglas County Historical Society

William Eads—Laborer

William Eads's journey to Oregon began in the cotton fields of South Carolina. Born a plantation slave, Eads remembered being raised by a black woman and "toiling under the lash among Negroes in the corn and cotton fields."

William Eads was an African American who, like so many other settlers, came to Oregon looking to begin a new life. Unlike so many other settlers who came to Oregon, William had to contend with the issue of bigotry. One hundred and fifty years ago, a black person could hardly find a place to call home in Oregon. William Eads's story is one of fierce courage, patriotism, and loyalty.

Work for William Eads started out harshly. An article written in 1901 by someone going by the name Umpqua claims that in South Carolina Eads was "overworked, illy fed and clothed, bowed 'neath the weights of great loads till his body grew crooked and misshapen." These grueling working conditions were not William's first difficult trial, and he overcame them as he did the others.

Life as a Soldier

When the Mexican-American War began in 1846, William Eads escaped the plantation and enlisted in the army under the name of William Williams. His owner came searching for him but his new comrades in arms hid William and "drove the master away with threats." As a soldier, he served under General Taylor, and participated in the storming of Monterey and the battle of Cerro Gordo.

William Eads liked the Army well, and the newspaper article from 1901 that told of his harsh working conditions in South Carolina also goes on to say of his military service that "he…was as loyal and true a patriot as ever wore the Army blue, devotedly loved the flag, which to the escaped slave was a real symbol of liberty."

This loyalty led William Eads to volunteer to replace federal troops maintaining posts in Oregon. After his discharge, he mined for a time in California and then came back to Oregon in the 1860s, settling a homestead on Thief Creek in Douglas County.

It's likely that William was able to obtain a homestead because he appeared to be a white man. This would have made all the difference, because in the Oregon of the 1850s only Caucasians could own land, and this left many African-Americans literally out in the cold.

Lawmakers continued to debate and pass legislation against blacks. One law called for an annual poll tax of $5.00 (the same law William Hunt Wilson voted against), and another prohibited marriages between whites and anyone of more than one-quarter black heritage.

Despite this atmosphere, William Eads served honorably in Company K, First Regiment of Oregon Infantry during the Civil War. His

William Eads—courtesy Douglas County Museum

headstone displays this military affiliation. After the war, he returned to his property on Thief Creek. Perhaps because of his light color, or maybe due to his hardworking nature, "Bill" Eads found work around Yoncalla splitting rails, clearing land, and doing other farm-type jobs.

One of the families William Eads worked for was that of William Hunt Wilson. When William Eads sold his homestead and lost most of his money in the 1870s, it was the Wilson family that took him in.

He lived with the Wilsons for the rest of his days. He tended the chickens and gathered eggs from the nests the hens had hidden in the barn. He also worked in the family's large garden, and cut wood and brush to help clear land and provide fuel for cooking and heating.

William Eads died on December 16, 1900. The government supplied his headstone, like it did for many who served their country in the military. The Wilson family buried him, not in a military cemetery, but in their own family plot.

Hispanics In Oregon

The history of the Latino presence in Oregon dates years prior to statehood. In fact, until the end of the Mexican-American War in 1848, the Mexican border lay just south of Ashland. In the early 1800s, Latinos in Oregon worked as miners, mule-packers, and cowboys (or *vaqueros*). Despite discrimination, Latinos continued to live and work here as railroad- and canal-builders, and as laborers on many farms around the state.

Men like Joaquin "Chino" Berdugo and Prim Ortega spent years as foremen at the P Ranch in Harney County. Prim earned $100.00 a month, making him the highest paid member of the P Ranch crew.

Life as a *vaquero* in the high deserts of Oregon followed a seasonal pattern. Since there were no fences, ranches joined together to round up scattered cattle. A crew of *vaqueros* and a chuck wagon (which carried supplies and provisions for cooking) from each ranch would round up and then separate the cattle according to their brands. New cattle would be branded, and then the men would drive their respective herds to summer ranges. At the close of the summer, the *vaqueros* would help select the very best cattle to be driven to market and sold.

In the winter, only the permanent crew stayed on. They watched over the herds in the lower elevations and helped the cattle weather the difficult winter storms by feeding them stored hay while the snow covered their natural forage.

Chinese in Oregon

In 1849 there were fewer than one hundred Chinese people in Oregon. That all changed with the growth of two industries in Oregon: mining and fish processing. The Chinese began coming to Oregon from the California gold fields around 1851. When opportunities in mining declined, they stayed in Oregon and found work in other occupations around the state.

Many Chinese who came to Oregon were men who had left families back in their homeland. Even in 1880, the Astoria census listed 2,316 Chinese men and only twenty-five women. It was many years before a second generation of Oregon-born Chinese came along.

Mining

In 1850s-era Oregon, mining was a major economic activity. Gold mining was underway in Baker and Grant Counties, while coal mining was taking place in Coos County. The 1860 census counted 1,793 miners in Oregon. Hundreds of people from California traveled to Oregon's Rogue River Valley and southern coast to join the gold rush that began with a gold strike in Jackson County in the early 1850s.

At first, most of the mining was done by panning in streams, sluicing water through a small channel, or shooting water at high pressures against hillsides (a process called placer mining) to dislodge gold nuggets and flakes. Eventually these methods gave way to looking directly for the nuggets, which were buried deep within the mountains themselves. Large quantities of money were needed in order to dig vertical shafts down to lode claims.

Hydraulic mining operations on the Baker County placer mine of Sheriff Harvey K. Brown, ca 1895—courtesy Oregon Historical Society—OrHi39332

Quartzville Mine, ca 1890—courtesy Oregon State Library

Gold Mine near Sumpter, Oregon, in 1890—courtesy Oregon Historical Society—OrHi21492

This changed mining from an individual to a corporate endeavor, but still left opportunities open for those willing to work extra hard.

Mining required long hours of hard work, digging up and panning gravelly soil, or digging shafts and tunnels into mountains. A major part of the latter job was moving boulders with poles and slings. The difficulty and danger of the work often led to injury and illness. Miners who worked under a contract typically had no sick-leave benefits. If a miner had to take time off due to illness or injury, his contract deadline was extended, and he would have to continue to work until he fulfilled it.

When the mining claims became less profitable, miners shifted to other work such as farming, ranching, and canning.

Chinese Miners in Oregon

Many of the miners who came to Oregon's gold rush early on were of Chinese origin, and racial tensions sometimes arose between them and immigrants of European ancestry. Many of the Chinese who traveled to America in search of gold came from the province of Guangdong. Economic hardship led many to jump aboard ships bound for the western United States, counting on promises of riches. They left behind wives and children, planning to return for them after striking it rich.

Gin Lin

Gin Lin—Mine Boss—courtesy Oregon Historical Society—OrHi21973

One such man with a dream was Gin Lin. Gin arrived in Oregon and set about mining the Applegate Valley of southern Oregon near Jacksonville. Asian miners were discriminated against both culturally and legally, which kept them from competing for the best mining claims. They would often have to wait until an impatient American miner had abandoned his claim, and then collect dust and flecks of gold that were left behind.

Gin became a contract labor broker, which meant he negotiated terms of labor for a crew that worked on one-time projects. He and his employees worked claims on the Applegate River for twenty years. Rumor has it that Gin made over a million dollars in profits from his mining operation. He sent back to China for his wife and family, and was often seen riding around Jacksonville in a horse-drawn buggy, visiting with many of the upper-class residents of the city.

Gin's story of success has a sad ending, however. After he returned to China in 1894, Gin was beaten to death in a robbery.

Early in the state's history, Oregon's economy revolved primarily around agriculture, and secondarily around mining, as well as the activities that supported these two industries. Timber and fishing were not yet the major contributors to the economy they would become in later years. In the 1860 census, less than 1 percent of the 18,370 workers with occupations were listed as lumbermen, sawyers, or woodcutters.

However, settlers engaged in other occupations did cut down many trees to clear land and build homes. Similarly, the fishing industry in Oregon employed only twenty-six fishermen in 1860, but there were certainly more people who took advantage of the abundant fisheries in Oregon's rivers and along the coast. Further, both of these industries grew significantly in the years leading up to the end of the century.

Bucking a spruce log in Tillamook County, ca late 19th century—courtesy Oregon State Library

Merchants

Immigrants to Oregon made many of the things they needed from local materials, but some things they wanted were not made locally. Merchants imported these items—typically through connections in San Francisco—and distributed them throughout the region. They also shipped locally made products to San Francisco, extended credit to farmers, speculated on land, and invested in local industries. By 1860, Oregon had 455 general merchants and storekeepers, as well as fifty-five traders and similar numbers of specialty merchants selling particular lines of products such as meat, bread, and shoes.

Portland's location at the confluence of the state's two largest navigable rivers made it the center of merchant activity. In the early 1850s, four young merchants from the East Coast set up shop on Front Street in Portland. Within a few years more merchants from New England established businesses in the city. Other parts of Oregon also had merchants, as shown by the story of John West.

Merchant, Millwright, and Canner—John West

John West worked as a sawmill foreman in Canada for fifteen years until word of the California gold rush reached Quebec. The spring and summer of 1849 found John sailing fifteen thousand miles around South America—a journey that would take months. His plan was to bring goods to sell to newly rich gold miners in San Francisco.

John West—courtesy James Aalberg

That plan didn't pan out so well. John found San Francisco to be an unruly boomtown that was in the process of growing from six thousand to twenty-one thousand people in just one year. Disappointed in San Francisco, he was open to new possibilities. It's likely that John was convinced to go to Oregon by Clement Adams Bradbury, who came to San Francisco on behalf of Clatsop County sawmill owners. John boarded the steamship S.S. Gold Hunter and arrived in Portland on December 1, 1850.

By July, John had left Portland (which had a population of around eight hundred then), and headed down the Columbia River to Astoria, a place more like those he was used to from his days on the St. Lawrence River. At that time, Astoria was a small town of about two hundred and fifty people, with just a few acres set aside for houses. Near the mouth of the Columbia River, Astoria is perched on forest-covered hillsides, and is reminiscent of San Francisco with its waterfront and steep streets. There, the forty-year-old John West worked as a millwright (a carpenter who also has knowledge of the gears and other machinery that run wind- and watermills), and lived in a boarding house along with twelve other boarders working as lumbermen.

John's next job was to supervise the construction of the Astoria Mills sawmill. The deal was to pay him $10.00 a day, plus room and board. Unfortunately, John did the work but wasn't paid. He ended up suing the men who hired him and won a judgment of $1,380.17 plus $62.82 in costs from a jury in U.S. District Court.

What's interesting about this lawsuit is that we learn from its documents what some things cost in the frontier town of Astoria in the 1850s. Tobacco cost $0.50, a bar of soap cost the same, and a pair of boots set John back $15.00. That might not seem like much money, but that same amount of tobacco would cost around $15.00 in today's dollars, and the boots would be well over $400.00. These prices were also high compared to those for the same goods on the East Coast.

Why were prices so high? Transportation costs, mostly. Goods created in Oregon were less expensive than those that had to be imported. And since Oregon was such a new place, there simply weren't many goods produced here yet.

A New Home

In November of 1853 John took an important step. He traveled to Oregon City and filed an application for a Donation Land Grant of 640 acres. John chose land about twenty-eight miles upriver from Astoria, which he found while canoeing the Columbia from Portland to Astoria, accompanied by a guide from the Clatsop tribe.

John had to work a second job while he developed his claim. He built and ran a sawmill in Oak Point, Washington (about fourteen miles west of Longview) for George Abernathy. In his spare time, John built his own water-powered sawmill. He also built a small log cabin to live in while constructing the mill. After five years of working on his claim and on the two sawmills, John completed both.

John West's Sawmill

It's impressive that John West could design, engineer, acquire raw materials for, and then build something as complicated as a sawmill. But he was determined to succeed in the business and—possessing the mind of an engineer and the tenacity of a pioneer—he was able to accomplish the task.

John's mill had a waterwheel with a diameter of somewhere between twenty and thirty feet, built over a fair-sized waterfall on a creek. Large oaken cogs on the waterwheel connected it to the mill. The cascading water put so much pressure on the cogs that they wore out in less than a week.

The waterwheel turned a crankshaft, which in turn moved a ripsaw up and down, cutting only on the downstroke. John would place a log into the saw using a ratchet arrangement called a rag- or sprocket-wheel. With each cut, John had to move the log into place using a crowbar. Despite the mill's pre–Industrial Revolution nature, John could cut fifteen hundred feet of lumber in a day working by himself.

Finally, in 1857, John brought his family from Quebec to the claim. The area would eventually be called Westport—named after John himself. The family stayed in John's crude log cabin, which was chinked with moss, mud, and grass. Although it was a little disconcerting, the Clatsop tribal members who would push the moss out of the cracks at night so they could get a peek at the newcomers were friendly.

As John's lumber business flourished, they were soon able to build a larger home. A thousand board feet of cut lumber would net John $100.00. A buyer from San Francisco later said that timber from John's area was the finest Douglas fir (called yellow fir at the time) available on the West Coast. Sailing ships came twice a year from the San Francisco Bay to pick up lumber and supply goods for John's new mercantile.

John West's Store

Not content with just cutting lumber, John opened a store. He completed it in 1858 to serve local residents, millworks, loggers, farmers, and fishermen. It's a good thing he diversified. Despite the fact that John added capacity by putting in two more waterwheels, a large drop in lumber prices between 1855 and 1860 cut his profits significantly. The store John opened later became a post office, with John as the postmaster.

Industrial Workers in 1860	
343	Blacksmiths
58	Saddlers
49	Harness-makers
32	Ship-carpenters
31	Machinists
98	Millers
63	Millwrights
35	Tanners
39	Tinsmiths
21	Gunsmiths
7	Watch-makers

The home of John West—courtesy James Aalberg

John's store was a two-story building partially built on pilings out on the Columbia River slough. Goods for the store came from the Allen and Lewis Company of Portland. Part of running a store in those days was extending credit to customers. Not everyone paid on time, and the Clatsop and Columbia County courthouses contain numerous records of John's attempts to collect on bad debts. Unfortunately, John's store burned to the ground on Christmas Day 1882. John later rebuilt and reopened the store, which stayed in business for many years afterwards.

John West's Cannery

John West's most enduring contribution was not in lumber or merchandising, but in doing something with all the fish caught in the Columbia River, which ran next to his property. He opened what was called a salterie, where he salted salmon, packed them in barrels, and then shipped them to California, the East Coast, and England.

At first, salting was a one-person operation. He cut the salmon in two long slices lengthwise, piled them into a large cask, and poured salt brine over them. This process preserved the salmon so it could be shipped over long distances on slow-moving ships. The process worked, but not well, and John was not satisfied with the quality of the product when it reached the market.

John West's Oregon Brand canned salmon label—courtesy James Aalberg

Salmon seining (a type of net that draws closed like a purse string), Columbia River, ca 1900—courtesy Oregon State Library

Always the entrepreneur and inventor, John set about finding better ways to preserve salmon. He opened the first cannery on the Oregon side of the Columbia River. It later became known by its most famous brand—John West Oregon Brand Fresh Columbia Salmon. Women working in the cannery earned $1.50 for a ten-hour day, while men earned $2.50 for the same work, as equal pay laws had not yet been established.

Working in a Cannery

All the work in the cannery was done by hand. Twenty men, two women, and two children worked in the plant at one time, as this was before laws prohibiting child labor. The workers used tinner's tools to crimp tops on the cans before putting them into a cooker. Afterwards, they would poke a hole in the tops of the cans, allowing steam to escape. The little holes were filled, and the cans were cooked a second time by steaming them for an hour.

After this, the cans were submerged in diluted lye, rinsed under a cold-water shower, and left to stand overnight on the cannery floor. The next morning the cans were dipped in a vat of varnish, labeled, boxed up, and shipped out.

Much of the cannery's labor force consisted of Chinese immigrants who began flooding into Astoria in the 1870s. At one point, more than two thousand Chinese laborers worked in the canneries of Astoria, cutting, sorting, canning, and later running the iron chink which automated the canning process and ultimately contributed to a decline in the demand for Chinese labor. The iron chink was marketed as a replacement for Chinese workers, with even its name derived from a derogatory term for the Chinese. It was directly linked to the U.S. government's Chinese Exclusion Act of 1882, which placed a ten-year moratorium on Chinese laborers entering the country, and made it illegal for those already here to obtain U.S. citizenship. Discrimination against Chinese labor stemmed partly from the belief that they were enabling employers to keep wages low. Immigration and labor continues to be a controversial topic today.

Harvesting Salmon

The demand for canned salmon didn't abate at all. The demand was so great, in fact, that new ways to "mine" the salmon from the Columbia were developed. Equipment included fish traps, seines (nets that hang vertically in the water with floaters and sinkers on either side, catching

Chinese workers clean fish in a salmon plant in Astoria ca 1880s—courtesy Clatsop County Historical Society

Westport city—courtesy James Aalberg

An "Iron Chink" processes canned salmon at an Astoria salmon plant, date unknown—courtesy Clatsop County Historical Society

fish when the sides are pulled together), and gill nets (aptly named nets designed to catch fish by their gills), but the fishwheels proved to be the most ingenious—and destructive. These water-powered nets automatically scooped up salmon and funneled them into the wheel before dropping them into a holding bin. These methods were so efficient that catches of Chinook salmon peaked by 1883, leading to massive declines of salmon populations early in the next century. Salmon canning was no small business. Output from the cannery in 1870 included 158,680 cans of salmon, valued at $27,188.00—a huge sum of money at the time.

Westport had a population of about one hundred fifty in the mid 1870s, but that ballooned to three hundred fifty during the canning season, mostly with Chinese labor working for John West's cannery.

In the 1880s John took advantage of blackberry bushes encroaching on Westport by employing men, women, and children to pick and deliver the luscious fruit to his cannery, where they were hermetically sealed and marketed. He also canned beef and mutton, which provided more for his employees to do during the off-season, when the salmon were not available to can.

In the late 1880s, John sold his company, though exactly how the brand and the equipment changed hands is unclear. The Liverpool, England, trading company that bought it was later acquired by Unilever, and then sold to the H.J. Heinz Company in 2000. John West Foods remains in Liverpool today as one of the world's largest marketing companies in canned goods, particularly canned fish. The John West brand of canned fish is the volume leader in the United Kingdom.

Mail stagecoach at Prineville, ca 1900—courtesy Oregon State Library

Merchant—John Sutherland

When Wallace Shortridge announced he was closing his post office in the city of Amos, John Sutherland began planning. Without a post office, the fifteen families living there would have to travel twelve miles south to Elkhead, or fourteen miles north to Cottage Grove to pick up their mail. John decided he could reopen the post office and make some extra cash at the same time.

John built a lean-to (a small building built up against another structure) against a barn to house the post office and store. It was only ten-by-fifteen feet, with a small five-by-five foot cubicle in the back to sort the mail. He ordered ninety dollars' worth of groceries on a ninety-day consignment from Mr. Beal, a salesman at Wadham and Kerr. He purchased one-hundred-pound sacks of sugar and fifty-pound sacks of flour, which he set on the floor and leaned against the wall. He also had barrels of beans and of other staples, such as Star and Climax tobacco, which he placed on shelves.

John enlisted the help of his thirteen-year-old daughter Emma, teaching her how to be assistant postmaster and clerk in his new store. Emma stood at the homemade counter and helped her father label the merchandise so she could remember how much things cost. They kept the change in a cigar box and wrote down every purchase. After practically no time at all, the little store and post office at Amos officially opened. John always extended credit to his customers and always closed on Sundays. But if someone came by and had no bread, he would give them a loaf from his own kitchen.

Some sales figures from the store included two hogs for $4.00, two sacks of flour for $2.00, eleven and a half pounds of bacon for $0.81, and a song book for $0.50. Mail came from Cottage Grove twice a week, along with more goods for the store. In the four years the Amos Post Office stayed open (before John built a bigger store in nearby London, Oregon), John Sutherland made only $71.32.

Oregon's First Resort — Merchant Philip Foster

Philip was thirty-eight years old when he came to Oregon from Calais, Maine, in 1842. He was accompanied by his wife, Mary Charlotte Pettygrove, and the rest of the Pettygrove family (who went on to help start the city of Portland—naming it for their hometown of Portland, Maine, after winning a coin toss). When they arrived, there weren't many people in the Oregon Territory. Some immigrants, including Philip, came by ships sailing around Cape Horn. A journey like that could take a year or more—if a ship could be found at all. Philip and his party had to wait twice for transportation—once in Lima, Peru, and earlier in a place called the Sandwich Islands (now Hawaii).

It would be more than one hundred years before the Sandwich Islands would become a part of the United States, but they were already an important trading center, and Philip benefited from his time there. While enjoying the warm tropical weather, he made contact with several distributors and merchants. These relationships paid off nicely for him once he arrived in the Oregon Territory.

Philip arrived in Oregon City in April of 1843, full of enthusiasm for starting his business. The smell of freshly cut lumber soon filled the air near the Willamette River ferry at the foot of Third Street as Philip and his partner built on a town lot they had bought from Dr. John McLoughlin. Their three-story building housed the Pettygrove Emporium, which opened for business in late May of 1843. The store occupied the ground floor, the Pettygroves the second, and Philip and his family lived on the third. Soon the doors to the store swung open regularly as residents of Oregon City came to admire some of the four thousand dollars' worth of inventory imported from the Sandwich Islands.

Though it was a success, Philip didn't stay at the store. He left it in the capable hands of his brother-in-law Francis Pettygrove, and moved his family to Eagle Creek in 1847. He acquired 824 acres from a man by the name of Samuel McSwain. Philip paid Mr. McSwain $100.00 to stop squatting on the land so that Philip could apply for a Donation Land Grant, which he received in 1867. Eventually the land claim was reduced to the standard 640 acres accorded to a husband and wife.

Sam Barlow — public domain photo

Road Builder

Though Philip now had a claim to tend, a very intriguing job offer came along that he couldn't turn down. A man named Sam Barlow approached Foster with a business proposition. Barlow had survived a harrowing journey across the shoulder of Mount Hood to Eagle Creek, and the experience had left him wanting to build a much-needed road there—an alternate route to the treacherous journey down the Columbia River by raft that most settlers were making at the time.

The agreement was very informal—written on a single piece of paper ripped from a ledger book. On the top of the page three lines written in pencil formed the contract between Foster and Barlow to build the Mount Hood Toll Road (known today as the Barlow Road). Philip provided the financial backing and a crew of forty men who hacked out the narrow trail through a hundred and fifty miles of forests, rivers, and marshy meadows from Oregon City to The Dalles, while Barlow provided the knowledge of the route the road would need to traverse.

In return for building the road, Philip collected tolls from anyone using it, charging $5.00 per wagon and $0.10 a head for livestock. From anyone who couldn't afford the toll, Philip took payment in trade; he collected rifles, blankets, or whatever they had to barter. Widows traveled for free, as did Native Americans (as the road crossed their land anyway). Philip and his sons ran the Barlow Road until 1865.

Farmer, Store Owner, and Restaurateur

Back on his 640 acres, Philip grew hay, harvested fruit such as peaches and apples, and raised beef. The immigrants coming along the Barlow Road arrived hungry, thirsty, and in need of provisions. In light of this, it was only natural for Philip to take on yet another role—that of restaurateur. Philip used the resources already at hand—crops from his farm and materials imported from his contacts in the Sandwich Islands—to supply people's needs and feed them right at his own dining room table.

Philip's store stocked things arriving families would need: liquor, socks, and other items. Prices were high, and some of the ten thousand immigrants who passed by "Foster's Place" bristled at the cost of goods. What they didn't understand was that the prices were high to offset the cost of importing many of the items from overseas (at prices higher than today's in absolute dollars).

To keep the store stocked, Philip relied on ships that would come up the Columbia River and stop at Vancouver. Since John McLoughlin served as Chief Factor of the Columbia Fur District for the Hudson's Bay Company, he could easily bring goods up the Willamette by small boat to Oregon City where Foster would pick them up.

Foster charged $0.50 for a meal, usually consisting of beef, potatoes, and carrots, which patrons ate on tin plates. One man was so hungry that he sat through three meals in a row. He wanted to eat a fourth, but the Fosters refused him. The man then went outside and writhed in pain because he had already eaten too much. He was ultimately okay, though.

Philip Foster as a younger man—courtesy Oregon Historical Society—OrHi3448

Some pioneers were not so lucky. One wagon train arrived at the farm in September, just before the peaches were ripe. Nancy Black and her cousin Mary, both only eight years old, had eaten very poorly on the journey. They got so excited to see fruit on trees that they picked peaches out of the orchard. They ate so many that by the next morning both had died. The two cousins were buried somewhere on the farm, but no one today knows where.

A Makeshift Hotel

Aside from the store and the restaurant, Philip also offered something else the immigrants needed: accommodations. Immigrants usually came in September, October, and November of each year, when the weather was getting colder. During those busy months, the Fosters served home-cooked meals and offered cabins for rent. Sometimes it was so busy that the family even rented out sleeping space on their parlor floor.

Accommodations were thus somewhat makeshift and not always ideal. Esther Belle Hanna found it so when she stayed at the farm, in one of the cabins. She stayed on one side of a double cabin, separated by a breezeway, known as a "dog trot." She describes it as "logs without caulking, windows without sashes, doors without hinges, and fireplaces without chimneys. But it didn't matter because the smoke just went out the cracks in the walls." She also writes in her well-known diary of a man dying of cholera, staying just fifteen feet away on the other side of the cabin. Recently a family came back to the now historic Philip Foster Farm claiming to be descendants of that man. They put up a symbolic grave marker at the site.

The Foster Family Grows

Philip and Charlotte Foster ran a farm, a store, a restaurant, and a hotel, but still found time to raise a family. Their daughter Lucy married Josiah Burnett in 1857. Josiah was a surveyor for the federal government. He surveyed areas around Eagle Creek, Roseburg, and the mouth of the Deschutes River.

In the spring of 1859, just after Oregon became a state, Philip Foster wrote to his son-in-law asking him to move back from Roseburg to Eagle Creek, a rural agricultural area near the Clackamas River. In the letter, Philip offered Josiah forty acres of land and told him of other parcels for sale nearby.

Josiah moved his family and built a house, keeping a list of items it took to complete the job. The total amounted to only $199.07. To outfit his new place, Josiah purchased, among other things, a soup tureen for $5.00, a water pitcher for $1.25, and a chamber pot for $2.50.

During the 1840s and '50s thousands of families packed their entire lives into small wagons, and fought their way over two thousand miles despite rough terrain, swollen rivers, broken axles, sickness, and hunger—all in an effort to find a new life in what they thought of as an unclaimed paradise called Oregon. If it weren't for Philip Foster,

Josiah and Lucy Burnett—courtesy of Joanne Broadhurst

This is the first page of a letter Philip Foster wrote to Josiah Burnett, asking him to move his family up to the Eagle Creek area—courtesy Tom Burnett and Joanne Broadhurst

those pioneer families on the last stretch of the Oregon Trail would have found reaching their goal even more difficult. Foster not only built a better route at the end of the Oregon Trail and helped thousands with food and shelter, but he also left an indelible mark on the state's history.

Philip Foster died of a heart attack on March 17, 1884—a few days after collapsing at the kitchen door shortly after lunch. Both his farm and a re-creation of his store, the first destination resort in the Oregon Country, still exist today as the Philip Foster Farm. It is owned and run by the Jackknife-Zion-Horseheaven Historical Society, with volunteer assistance from descendants of Philip himself— Tom Burnett and Joanne Broadhurst. Read their story on page 165.

Conclusion

In just fifty years Oregon was transformed from a territory into a state, from a place with fewer than twelve thousand residents to one with over four hundred thousand. The jobs Oregonians performed changed radically as well, from a focus primarily on farming to one moving in the direction of manufacturing, transportation, trade, and services. While the number of farmers and farm laborers grew more than fivefold from 1860 to 1900, the number of people in other occupations grew more than twelvefold. Rapid advances in machines and electricity were to bring even more major changes in the following fifty years.

Worker tests the moisture content of Douglas fir, ca 1930s—courtesy Oregon State Library

Section Two

1900–1950

Introduction

June 19, 1901 was a landmark day for Arthur Gardner. It was the beginning of his first full day as a married man. It was also the day he began keeping daily records of his home and work lives in a journal. Arthur wrote in his journals for nearly three decades. They record Arthur's hopes and aspirations to succeed in work, and the many frustrations he encountered along the way when jobs didn't pan out.

In many ways, Arthur's struggles at the beginning of the twentieth century mirror those of people in the beginning of the twenty-first. Oregon's population was growing, which resulted in more business and industry, providing more opportunities to work and raise a family. However, with more people came more competition, and often Arthur searched for weeks at a time without finding a job. Repeatedly, he had to settle for undesirable work that at least paid something, rather than going on with no salary at all. Arthur's full story is on page 100.

A Growing Oregon

Many things had changed in Oregon between the mid-1800s and the turn of the century. The amount of mining decreased. The salmon-canning industry grew, and then declined. Cattle ranching grew east of the Cascades. Transcontinental railroads arrived, spurring the expansion of railroad lines within Oregon. Wheat

Arthur Gardner poses with his new wife, Nellie May, June 21, 1900—courtesy Christy Van Heukelem

Unloading salmon, Columbia River, ca 1930s—courtesy Oregon State Library

Top Occupations in 1900			
1	Farmers	34,297	20%
2	Non-farm laborers	20,937	12%
3	Farm laborers	17,316	10%
4	Servants and waiters	7,310	4%
5	Merchants, dealers, hucksters, and peddlers	5,679	3%
6	Miners and quarrymen	5,154	3%
7	Carpenters and joiners	4,357	3%
8	Steam railroad employees	4,057	2%
9	Teachers and college professors	3,495	2%
10	Draymen, hackmen, teamsters, etc.	3,443	2%
11	Salesmen and saleswomen	3,365	2%
12	Clerks, copyists, stenographers, and typewriters	3,170	2%
13	Stock raisers, herders, and drovers	3,142	2%
14	Fishermen and oystermen	2,756	2%
15	Saw- and planing mill employees	2,449	1%

farming and sheep ranching expanded. The timber industry grew. Oregon's population—especially in urban areas—grew dramatically as well, especially in the early 1890s. In only ten years, from 1900 to 1910, the state's population grew almost 63 percent—three times as much as the nation's. This meant an additional 259,229 people in the state.

Another important development at the beginning of the century was legislation that put into place the eight-hour workday. In 1908, the U.S. Supreme Court upheld Oregon's restriction on the working hours of women to a maximum of ten hours per day. By 1910, the union movement had won an eight-hour day for skilled union workers in Portland. Oregon passed laws limiting work to an eight-hour workday for public works in 1912 and for women workers in 1914.

Farming

Seventeen out of twenty people with listed occupations in the 1910 census were men. As in 1860, farming was the most common job in the state. Two of five men with occupations were either farmers or farm laborers "working out" at another's farm.

Oregon had almost 78,000 workers on farms and in gardens, orchards, and pasturelands in 1910. There were 45,502 farms in Oregon, averaging almost 257 acres each. Farms covered about one-sixth

Workers picking hops—courtesy Oregon Historical Society—Drake 3434

1909 Average Annual Incomes
Average of All Industries $544.00
Finance, Insurance, and Real Estate $1,263.00
Clerical Workers, Manufacturing, and Steam Railroads $1,136.00
Federal Employees, Executive Departments $1,106.00
Construction Trades, Union Workers $1,086.00
Postal Employees $948.00
Ministers $831.00
Bituminous Coal Mining $751.00
Nonprofit Organization Workers $741.00
State and Local Government Workers $696.00
Street Railway Workers $671.00
Steam Railroads, Wage Earners $644.00
Telegraph Industry Workers $622.00
Gas and Electricity Workers $618.00
Wholesale and Retail Trade Workers $561.00
Public School Teachers $476.00
Domestic Servants $420.00
Farm Labor $328.00
Medical/Health Services Workers $326.00

Men working a flax-harvesting machine in Marion County in 1940—courtesy Oregon State Library

Women picking strawberries in Silverton, ca 1942—courtesy Oregon Historical Society—Drake 3037

of the state. Hired managers and tenant farmers worked on some of these farms, but the landowners themselves farmed on more than three-quarters of them.

Most farms included horses, dairy cows, and chickens, and many also had cattle, swine, or both. Many also kept beehives. However, the most common farm animal was sheep. Only 15 percent of farms reported that they kept sheep, but there were almost 2.7 million sheep on those farms, making them even more numerous than the state's 1.75 million chickens. Shearing sheep, collecting eggs, and milking dairy cows were major activities. In 1909, Oregon's farms produced about twenty-four pounds of sheep's wool, eighteen-dozen eggs, and eighty-three gallons of milk for every person in the state.

Wheat and oats were the most common crops, followed by hay and forage. Potatoes were also very common, with an average of one or two acres grown on more than half of the farms. Farmers also raised fruits—apples, plums, pears, and cherries were most popular—and other common crops included strawberries, raspberries, nuts, and hops.

Running a Dairy—Darrell Tagg

Darrell Tagg came to Oregon in 1910. He married into the Morrison family of Oregon pioneers and bought the Morrison farm for $1.00. For Darrell, clearing land for farming by cutting down trees and pulling out roots was a constant chore. He was a very progressive farmer, always looking for new equipment to help him farm better. Darrell soon started raising dairy cows and selling milk and fresh-cut beef to residents around Warrenton, which is located on the north Oregon coast.

A favorite family story says that one day, when Darrell was out selling quarts of milk for a quarter, he found a family that needed the milk, but couldn't afford it. Instead of giving them the milk, or providing them with credit, Darrel gave them a milk cow so they could have fresh milk whenever they needed it.

Darrell also regularly sold milk to an ice cream store in Astoria called Tagg's Ice Cream Parlor. Unfortunately, farming didn't pay very well for Darrell. He supplemented his income by founding Astoria Heavy Hauling and Tagg Motor Freight. He even took a job setting bowling pins for $1.00 a day.

Townsend Creamery workers in Portland in 1910—courtesy Oregon State Library

Farmer—Ed Carl

In the early 1900s, around the beginning of Oregon's second fifty years, Ed Carl found that the fertile land around Carlton gave him all he needed to raise dairy cows. Ed had to rise early to milk his Holsteins by hand. To feed all those cows, Ed raised hay and oats. It took a lot of practice to lead a team of work horses while perched a dozen or so feet on top of a wagon loaded with hay. It was worth it for Ed, though. He would take some of the cream and sell it to the new Carlton Rose Creamery. In turn, the creamery would package the cream and sell it to customers in the area. Ed had successfully continued the work started by his father.

Ed Carl—courtesy Austin Warner

Ed Carl riding a hay wagon around the farm—courtesy Austin Warner

Ed and Lulu Carl with young Austin—
courtesy Austin Warner

CORVALLIS GAZETTE-TIMES—
JUNE 22, 1945

Harvest Hands Badly Needed in All Benton Area: James A Carr, County Farm Labor Boss, Makes Special Plea Today

Strawberry pickers, hay harvest hands and other farm workers are urgently needed at this time, according to word received from James A. Carr, Benton county farm labor assistant. The recent warm weather brought on the strawberries so rapidly that many additional pickers are needed at once in order to avoid possible crop losses, says Carr.

Ed Carl's father, Wilson, had been an orphan. He came to Oregon and built a home, a family, and a community (see Wilson's story on page 21). Home must have been a big part of Ed's upbringing, because he spent his entire life on the farm his father bought in the town that now bears his name: Carlton. While Ed's brothers left the farm to open up mechanic's shops and work for lumber mills, Ed stayed to work the 575 acres at the foot of the Oregon coast range, about seven miles north of McMinnville.

The dairy was a large part of his farm, but not the only part. Apart from the dairy cows, Ed also had a large orchard of pears, apples, and plums. One of Ed's pear trees still stands on the property after 125 years. In addition to working the farm, Ed also took a job at the prune dryer nearby owned by Link Cummins.

The Prune Dryer

Willamette Valley plums were harvested in early September. Oregon's proximity to California, plus the introduction of the railroads, made it easy for Hispanic workers to travel north to Oregon for work on the farms. During the harvesting period, these workers lived in one-room shacks provided by orchardists. They picked the plums, put them into buckets, and then transported them to the dryer, which looked very much like an ordinary barn.

The dryers held large furnaces inside that used heat to transform plums into prunes. Working in the dryer, Ed would place plums

Pictured is a Twin Hills prune dryer (tunnel variety) on top of Ankeny Hill near Fairview School around 1920—courtesy Marion County Historical Society

Edwin Carl and family—courtesy Austin Warner

1909 Average Per Capita
Consumer Spending Nationwide

Food
$81.43

Housing
$61.48

Clothing
$30.00

Personal Business
$9.61

Recreation
$9.49

Religion/Charities
$9.05

Tobacco
$6.33

Local Transportation
$5.12

Private Education and Research
$4.59

Utilities
$4.00

Furniture
$3.25

Physicians
$3.24

Inter-City Transport
$2.97

Personal Care
$2.88

Auto Purchases
$1.85

Gas and Oil
$1.36

Telephone and Telegraph
$1.00

Dentists
$0.91

Auto Parts
$0.59

onto large wooden or wire racks, put them into the dryer, and then remove them when they had dried sufficiently. The dryers started out at around 120 degrees, but went up to 180 degrees over somewhere between twenty-four and forty-eight hours. Bringing the temperature up too quickly caused the fruit to split open. After Ed removed the trays, he likely put the prunes into bins or piles to sweat over the next one to three weeks.

Grading came next, when workers separated Ed's prunes according to the number required to make up a pound. Dipping them in boiling water and glycerin added color and killed insect eggs. The final step was to wrap the prunes in paper and pack them in boxes, ready for labels and shipment.

Most of the prunes grown in the area were Italian, or "purple plum" prunes. During this time, the Pacific Northwest produced some thirty million pounds of prunes each year. Prunes were a very inexpensive fruit and very popular.

When he wasn't milking, haying, or drying prunes, Ed loved to sit around the fireplace with his family in the home built by his father. He even had time to help teach a young man about working on a farm. That boy was his grandson, Austin Warner, who worked with his dad and later took over management of the dairy. You can read Austin's story on page 129.

"20,000 members of the Ladies Waist Maker's Union staged a three-month strike; they won most of their demands." "The International Ladies' Garment Worker's Union called a strike to protest poor working conditions and low wages."

"The Sixteenth Amendment to the Constitution, authorizing income taxes, was passed by Congress."

"A tobacconist convention that year protested the automobile; they were concerned that it would lure people away from homes and clubs and smoking would be diminished."

Source:
Quotes above from "Historical Snapshot – 1909" table in Working Americans: 1880 – 1999, Volume I: The Working Class, by Scott Derks, Grey House Publishing, Lakeville, CT, 2000, p. 106.

"127,731 automobiles were produced, twice the number of the previous year; the Ford Model T's production of 20,000 cars was the nation's top seller." "Nationwide, 34 states adopted a 25-mile-per-hour speed limit."

"Wilbur Wright designed an airplane for the U.S. Army that carried two passengers, flew for one hour, and reached a top speed of 49 miles per hour."

"Ice cream sales reach 39 million gallons, up from five million 10 years earlier."

Source:
Quotes above from "Historical Snapshot – 1909" table in Working Americans: 1880 – 1999, Volume II: The Middle Class, by Scott Derks, Grey House Publishing, Millerton, NY, 2001, p. 94.

Steam threshing near Eugene in 1901—courtesy Oregon State Library

Harvesting Wheat

Crews of fifteen to twenty-five men (even as many as forty) worked in dusty wheat fields with teams of as many as thirty-three strong horses or mules. These teams pulled equipment designed to assist them in their work, which was to till the soil, to plant the wheat, and later to harvest it. Wheat was Oregon's most common crop. At harvest time, many men worked in hot, dry weather to thresh the wheat, using either horse or steam power. Afterward, they filled and sewed shut the heavy sacks of grain by hand. After the sacks were sewn shut, the workers loaded them onto horse-drawn wagons for transport to the closest rail depot.

The horses, steam engines, and workers all required water, which was typically supplied by a horse-drawn wagon carrying a long wooden barrel. Cooks, usually two young women from the local community, worked hard to feed the crew of workers from a horse-drawn cookhouse on wheels. A cook's workday could stretch from 3 AM to 10 or 11 PM—an even longer day than that of the men. Bringing in the wheat harvest was a collaborative effort.

"No farm is an island." This was how the families that sowed and reaped around the small community of Wren, Oregon, expressed their interdependence. In 1909, Wren, a few miles west of Corvallis, consisted of a railroad section house, a church, a dancehall and tavern combined with a general store, and five or six houses surrounded by miles of farmland. A couple of miles outside of Wren stood the Harris place. Henry Harris's son George had taken over running the farm upon Henry's death in 1890.

George Harris is fourth from the right in this photo of the threshing of wheat, barley or oats in 1909—courtesy Elmer Harris Taylor

Wheat Farmer—George Harris

Like his father before him, George ran a sawmill, but closed it down in 1908 after a labor dispute. The workers wanted more money and went on strike. George simply closed the headgate where water ran into the mill and said, "We're out of business."

After closing the mill, George took his team of horses, Nig and Bolliver, out to do day labor. His real love, however, was farming. He had orchards and a large garden, but wheat was his main crop, and harvesting it at just the right time was crucial. In August, there were only seven to ten days after the wheat ripened before the crop was ruined. The hot summers from 1909 to 1911 caused George difficulties as he tried to time the harvest just right.

George's biggest problem, however, wasn't the weather. It was that he simply could not harvest all the wheat by himself. George and the farmers around Wren needed each other. One man could use a cradle or scythe to cut an acre a day, if he worked hard. A medium-sized field was too big for one man, but too small for the farmer to afford his own reaping and threshing equipment.

So George would bring his reaper-binder machine to harvest a farmer's wheat in return for labor on George's own threshing day. Harvesting was a community event. Each farmer took turns using George's McCormick brand reaper-binder, and everyone pitched in to help their neighbors.

Threshing was a loud, dangerous undertaking. It took three days to thresh George's wheat, two days for the next-smallest farms, and

George Harris pictured around 1923—courtesy Elmer Harris Taylor

one day each for the rest. The job required twenty horses and twenty-two men. Crews would lift the forty- or fifty-pound shocks (piled sheaves of grain placed upright for drying or ripening) of wheat onto a wagon, while dogs quickly caught field mice that had been hiding underneath.

Three men, called bundle pitchers, would pitch the shocks into the threshing machine, which chopped up the stems into short pieces of straw and separated the heads into grains. The machine shook violently and made such a loud noise that anyone working it would become dizzy. Things were no better at the other end, where the separator blew out straw and chaff in a constant, itchy stream.

The separator could thresh five hundred sacks of wheat in a day, each weighing around seventy pounds. For the farmers, the sacks of wheat were like sacks of money; they provided wealth, food, and security for the coming winter.

When it was time for a break, the farmers would rest in the shade or tip back in a chair to discuss whether to sell the wheat as grain or flour, and whether to sell it locally or haul it to market in Portland. Then it was back to the fields for hours more back-breaking work before the men would eat a hearty dinner and head off for the swimming hole to clean up as best they could.

At the conclusion of the harvest George calculated his expenses. He saved fifty sacks of oats (which George also grew) for the horses, two hundred sacks for the cows and sheep, and ten sacks for the chickens. The family would live on six sacks of flour, two sacks of rolled wheat, two sacks of cornmeal, and two sacks of rolled oats. That left him with two wagonloads of grain to sell.

George brought the grain to the gristmill in Albany and, unlike other farmers, waited for his grain to be ground into flour so that he could say, "This is our bread, from our own acres."

Running a Farm — Alice Hanley

Alice Hanley owned some of the best land outside the Willamette Valley. It was situated between Medford and Central Point in southern Oregon's Jackson County. Twenty acres of her father's original homestead were now hers—part of a split between her six brothers and sisters—and Alice was not about to waste it.

Raising cattle and hay was common, but Alice Hanley was no common farmer. Around 1920 she decided to do something no one had tried before—planting grass as a crop to produce seed.

Alice had heard about a variety of bluegrass that could be raised and harvested for seed. She was a pioneer of what would become an industry producing more grass seed than anywhere else in the world.

Alice's work wasn't confined to the farm, though. Her concerns over the influence of the Ku Klux Klan led her to run for the Oregon legislature in the 1920s. She lost, but her place on the ticket garnered plenty of attention, because the legislature was all male at the time. It would remain so until 1928, when Dorothy McCullough Lee won election as a state lawmaker.

Mining

Over five thousand Oregonians worked in mining in 1910. This made it one of Oregon's top industries. During this time, Charles Marshall worked as a mining engineer and surveyor on the R & S Gold Mine, along the Illinois River in Curry County.

Charles was a quartz, or "rock," miner. Rather than sift through sand and dirt in a streambed, panning for gold, Marshall dug shafts into the mountains. Marshall hoped one of these shafts would cut into a vein of gold, or into a deposit of gold ore. He kept a diary of his adventures in the mine, and it is rich in mining terms and descriptions of the difficult conditions he worked in.

Alice and Claire Hanley pictured on their farm near Jacksonville, Oregon, in the 1930s—courtesy Southern Oregon Historical Society

Weigh bill for hay sold from Alice Hanley's farm in 1907—courtesy Southern Oregon Historical Society

Miners working their claims in Jacksonville, January 31, 1932—courtesy Oregon Historical Society—OrHi57124

Portrait of Sam Palmer at Eagleton, Baker County, in 1902. On back of photo: "Old miner in front of cabin, soliloquizing on the 'big strike' he is about to make."—courtesy Oregon State Library

Oregonian — May 1, 1935

"Walkout Closes Two Sawmills: Clark & Wilson Plants Shut Down"

Swelling the ranks of striking workers from just 450 to 1150, 700 workers walked off the job at the Clark & Wilson Lumber Company mills in Linnton and Prescott after negotiations with mill executives once again proved unsuccessful. The walkout was peaceful and orderly, and completely shut down operations at both mills. Meanwhile, other Portland-area mills continued production as usual.

Thursday, January 3, 1907. We started the mill, but quit at noon. Trash clogged the screen in mill forebay and battery pipes repeatedly. At noon Higgins [his partner] turned water out of upper ditch. Rain and heavy wind all day—snow practically gone at dark. Creek was very high all day. It cut a new channel around bridge at old camp. At dark weather turned colder, and some snow fell.

Most small mines consisted of a single shaft. The only light in the shaft came from a lantern or candle. The smells of decaying lumber and powder smoke filled the shaft's chambers. The miners drilled small holes in the side of the shaft by hand, filled them with powder, and ignited the powder to blow out part of the rock. They would then shovel, or muck, the ore into buckets or cars, and raise or push it to the surface.

From Charles's description we know they had a mill on-site that worked to separate the ore from the gold, using water flowing through a screen. As hard as Charles worked, there is no record of him ever striking it rich.

Manufacturing

During the early twentieth century, farms made the transition from horse-drawn implements to farm tractors. Larger, more automated farms and cheaper agricultural products were made possible by the new technology. While this squeezed smaller farmers, new, attractive industries were growing. Between 1900 and 1928, Oregon's timber harvest grew fivefold. Although automation assisted that expansion, the number of logging and lumber mill jobs must have climbed rapidly as well. The Great Depression reduced this activity for about six years, but after that, rapid growth continued all the way to the mid-twentieth century. In the late 1930s, new hydroelectric dams on the Columbia River generated power enough to spawn an aluminum refining industry. Then, during the Second World War, Oregon's shipyards experienced enormous growth, pulling people to Oregon from around the country to build and repair the U.S. military's large ships. The first half of the twentieth century also saw Oregon's paper manufacturing industry add jobs, and its woolen- and linen-goods manufacturing industries wax and wane.

Thomas Lister Kay (front row, left) working at the Brownsville Woolen Mill—courtesy Mission Mill Museum

Thomas Kay Woolen Mill

Thomas Lister Kay was born in 1837, in Appleby, England. He began his career by working in the spinning department of Billy Denby's woolen factory. By the time Kay was thirteen years old, he had begun a full spinning apprenticeship.

After coming to America later in his life, Thomas Kay began looking for a site for his own mill. In 1888, he selected Salem, and purchased the old Pioneer Oil Company property and its water power. Then he began a campaign to raise a $20,000.00 subsidy from Salem's citizens, money which would supplement the $55,000.00 that Thomas Kay personally contributed. Salem's enthusiasm for the mill is reflected by the speed in which the money was raised. The $20,000.00 was pledged by 352 citizens in less than a month.

Seven years later, in 1895, the Thomas Kay Woolen Mill burned to the ground. The main mill structure was destroyed in less than two hours. Inadequate insurance increased the financial loss of the mill, but the citizens of Salem again demonstrated their enthusiasm by raising an additional $25,000.00 in one night. The employees were so proud to work in the Kay Mill that when the mill burned, many workers offered to donate a month's wages towards its reconstruction. As Thomas B. Kay III, explained, "To them it was an important part of living, as opposed to just a place to work."

From its earliest history, the manufacture of wool fabric has depended on the skill and ingenuity of the worker. Although ever

This is the original Thomas Kay Woolen Mill building, constructed in 1889. Sadly, it burned to the ground in 1895—courtesy Mission Mill Museum

The Thomas Kay Woolen Mill and its associated outbuildings in 1908—courtesy Mission Mill Museum

greater mechanization replaced production by hand, the creation of wool cloth remained labor-intensive, requiring careful attention to detail. The fact that mills used varying qualities of fleece and produced a variety of fabric types and weights demanded daily flexibility and versatility from the workers.

Unlike workers in some of the large and impersonal woolen mills of the East Coast, the employees of the Thomas Kay Woolen Mill shared a sense of camaraderie, considering their fellow workers a sort of family, and had a generally congenial relationship with the Kay family management. Workers often recruited friends, neighbors, and relatives, and frequently received their training from fellow mill workers.

The mill relied on the knowledge, abilities, and experience of key workers in each department, particularly the extensive experience of the founder, Thomas Lister Kay. The mill depended most on the mill superintendent, the wool grader, the dyemaster, and the finishing room boss. Other important jobs included the boss carder, the spinning boss, and the weave room boss. Some people in these key positions usually had lengthy prior experience in other mills and often some formal training. Others had worked for years in less skilled jobs at the Kay Mill and moved up as they gained the required knowledge. Decisions usually had to be made based on the handle, feel, smell, and look of the wool or the cloth. Working knowledge of these subtle sensory perceptions could be acquired only after years of experience.

While far from ideal by today's standards, wages, hours, and working conditions at the Kay Mill were considered good, or at least comparable to other mills and factories in the area, until at least the 1930s. During its early history, the mill operated six days a week in ten-hour shifts using men, women, and children. When government regulations required an eight-hour day in the 1930s, the mill complied, reducing hours per week and eliminating child labor. During World War II, when the Kay Mill produced significant quantities of cloth and blankets for the U.S. Army, shifts in some departments worked around the clock. Given the hazards of the machinery and the dangerous conditions created by slippery floors, acids, chemicals, and poor lighting, there were surprisingly few serious accidents, as workers learned to be careful. However, poor lighting and tremendous noise frequently produced sight and hearing problems.

Wool is manufactured from the fleece of sheep. Before fleece was sold to the mill, the sheep needed shearing. Shearing requires

Unknown mill worker sorting fleeces in the Mill's wool warehouse—courtesy Mission Mill Museum

The Overall Girls (or Coverall Girls as they were sometimes known) made the bold move during WWI to wear overalls rather than long dresses when they took over the machinery positions vacated by the men who were sent off to the front—courtesy Mission Mill Museum

skill, strength, and dexterity. The shearer had to remove the fleece from the sheep in one piece without injuring the animal. With the introduction of machine shears, run by a gasoline engine or electricity, shearing became faster and less arduous.

Fleeces were delivered to the mill's larger warehouse to be sold, weighed, and sorted. In order to make cloth of even texture, it was essential that fibers in the finished cloth be of similar length and coarseness. Sorting has changed less than any other process in the woolen industry and is done by hand even today; no way has yet been found to mechanize it.

The mill's dye house was used for several very important processes, most of which were required before the wool could be sent into the main building. Spinning and weaving required clean wool, but domestic raw wool contained an average of 60 to 65 percent foreign matter, so first the fleece was brought to the cone duster, where wool was fed into a rotating cylinder and spiked arms beat out the dirt and loosened the sticky "tags." Heavy dirt fell through the grid or screen walls of the cylinder, and light materials were blown out the exhaust by a fan. The wool was then washed in another machine, the scouring train. The water for this process came from the mill-race, a diversion of a stream for use in a factory or mill. The machine consisted of two parts: bowl-like containers, which were filled with warm water, soap, and alkali; and rakes, which moved the wool slowly through the water.

Wool fiber has great capacity to absorb dye with deep color and clarity. Both stock (dyeing the wool before spinning) and piece (dyeing the fabric after manufacture)

Steam drifts off of a Dye House vat while P.G. Olds and Harry Smith pole the wool to set the color—courtesy Mission Mill Museum

dyeing were central operations at the dye house. Dyes and chemicals were mixed by hand at the Kay Mill and had to be accurate to the gram. Dye formulas were complex and exacting, and accuracy and consistency of color were vital for the reputation of the mill and the marketing of the finished product. The dyemaster's job was one of the most important at the mill. He had to have both training and experience to assume the responsibilities of the position. The dyers were hardy, strong workers who dealt with difficult working conditions. The dye house was hot, steamy, wet, and smelly. Once used, the dye baths were commonly dumped directly into the millrace. The rumor around town was that you could tell the color of the fabric being made at the mill by the color of the millrace. Obviously, this practice is not permitted today.

Men took the cleaned, dried, and sometimes dyed wool to the picker house for picking and blending. Wool picking, rag picking, and mixing were all housed in the late-nineteenth-century brick picker house located just east of the main mill building. The unheated and poorly lit picker house created difficult conditions for the workers, who became accustomed to wearing multiple layers of clothing, straining their eyes in the shadowy vaulted spaces, and hurrying to the dye house to warm themselves during lunch time.

Spinning is the process of drawing out and twisting the wool to turn it into yarn. In early days, spinning was accomplished by using drop spindles. The introduction of the spinning wheel made drop spindles obsolete. One spinner with one spinning wheel could spin one pound of yarn per day. The creation of the

Mill employees in 1929. The Kay family was not the only family at the Mill. Several relatives worked together for generations, such as the Lehmans, the Reids, the Ohmarts, the Noaches, the Boedingheimers, and the Seamsters, all of which have family members posing for this photo—courtesy Mission Mill Museum

original spinning jenny, invented in 1764, allowed for the factory production of yarn. The machine used eight spindles. By turning a single wheel, the operator could spin eight threads at once. The thread that the spinning jenny produced was coarse and lacked strength. With the creation of the spinning mule, which spun 336 spindles at a time, production was increased while costs decreased as fewer spinners were needed.

Unlike other mill workers, who were paid by the hour, weavers were paid by piecework—that is, they were paid based on the amount and quality of finished goods. This was designed to help keep the quality of the goods high, and to enforce concern for the finished product.

The final process in making wool was finishing. Burlers found and removed knots, bunches, and loose ends on an elevated tabletop. They then entered a number, style number and date, and sent the cut to the menders.

The menders inserted yarn in the woven fabric where any warp threads were missing. Mending was very delicate and time-consuming work, generally done by women. Every missing thread had to be carefully handwoven into the piece of fabric so that it looked as if it had been machine woven. Menders sat on benches or in chairs by the window and pulled the fabric down over perches to see the marked imperfections and repair them. The fabric was then ready for the fulling mills.

Woolen cloth direct from the loom was coarse, loosely woven, dirty, and generally unattractive. The finishing processes made it soft, pliable, compact and attractive. Fulling is a vigorous working of woolen cloth in a solution of water and a thickening agent in order to cause felting and a controlled shrinkage. Felting is the interlocking of millions of individual wool fibers in the cloth. Fulled woolen cloth does not unravel easily because, in addition to the weave, felting has caused the fibers to cling to each other. The tendency of the wool fiber to felt is one of its natural attributes and is

Unknown employee adjusting a carding machine on the Mill's third floor—courtesy Mission Mill Museum

An "Overall Girl" operating one of the automatic looms—courtesy Mission Mill Museum

Thomas Kay Woolen Mill's bowling team. In addition to bowling, the Mill supported an employee baseball team and horseshoe club—courtesy Mission Mill Museum

encouraged by the warmth and pressure in the fulling operations. Shrinkage reduced the area of the cloth, and as a result the cloth became thicker and the weave tighter.

Moisture, friction, and heat are necessary for fabric to felt. A soap mixture introduced moisture, and friction was created by forcing the fabric through a series of rollers and traps, which in turn produced heat. The fabric had to be checked regularly and measured to determine whether it was shrinking correctly.

After washing and drying, machines brushed out the fibers. Finally the fabric was pressed, which brought out the texture, luster, and appearance desired in the finished fabric. Pressing demanded close attention to detail because it was the final process in the production of woolen and worsted fabrics. Heat, pressure, time, and moisture controlled pressing. Since all four of these factors could be varied, infinite combinations were used to create different fabrics.

The final check and evaluation of the fabric before it was readied for shipping was the job of the inspector. The inspector looked for imperfections, stains, and damage that may have occurred during finishing operations, and for unevenness of color. Any irregularity was marked with string on the selvage (the edge of a fabric that is woven so that it will not fray or ravel), and the customer was given a discount or yardage allowance for the imperfections. The inspector was required to have excellent eyesight and good judgment, as he had to pass or reject fabric based on its imperfections and variations in color.

The Thomas Kay Woolen Mill had to close its doors in 1962. The mill still stands, but bears the name Mission Mill Museum. The machines sit silent but appear not to have been touched since the last day of production. Photos of those who worked in the mill explain the process of turning fleece into wool. You can even spot someone's old lunch box sitting amongst the abandoned vats and looms.

Women at Work

Women working at Pacific Telegraph & Telephone—courtesy Oregon Historical Society—Gi9077-A

It was common for women to work in the early 1900s, but most of them worked at a wide variety of tasks in and around their own homes. Of the 230,914 women age ten or older, only about 18 percent had specific occupations. The most common of these was that of servant. There were 6,433 female servants in Oregon.

Women manufacturing dresses, ca 1916–1919 — courtesy Oregon Historical Society — OrHi28891

This occupation was especially common for young, single women. More than 6 percent of all women ages sixteen to twenty were servants. Men, too, filled the role of servant; there were 3,403 male servants in Oregon in 1910.

Servants

Having a servant was considered a sign of wealth and status. Although it was typical for a middle-class home to have at least one servant in other parts of the country, it was not very common in the Pacific Northwest (at least when compared to the Midwest and the East).

Servants worked long hours—sunrise to sunset and beyond. They had little time to socialize with their peers, and rarely went to the dance halls, ice cream parlors, or bars which the women who worked in factories frequented. They also had no place to entertain company. They tended to have lower wages (approximately $3.00 a week) because they received room and board.

While servants shared many of the same working conditions, they didn't necessarily share the same job duties. Servant is a general term that encompasses a variety of jobs. Servants were cooks, bakers, chambermaids, cleaning women, silver polishers, washwomen, and ironers. Families commonly hired an additional, part-time servant to do the laundering.

Christian Latta stands with his governess in Milwaukie, Oregon, date unknown — courtesy Oregon Historical Society — bao21570

Between the Civil War and World War I, conditions changed for servants. For instance, there was an expansion in job opportunities for women, allowing them to engage in a wider variety of occupations, which created a shortage in available servants. Also, domestic service work shifted from being a live-in occupation to a live-out occupation, and servants less often lived at the homes of those they served.

Teaching

Sewing room at Chemawa boarding school. A number of students are working on treadle sewing machines, some are handstitching, and a teacher is measuring a girl's dress. Next to the teacher is a table with a pattern laid out, ca 1900—courtesy Oregon State Library

In the 1900 census, 960 men and 2,535 women listed their occupation as teacher. Public education may have begun in Oregon mainly through the efforts of various missionary groups, but by the turn of the century the state legislature had become involved. They began regulating education by passing a law requiring teachers to meet certain standards.

In 1901, another law went into effect, requiring public high school education in all Oregon counties. This posed a problem in many areas of Oregon, where homes stood great distances from schoolhouses that were often run-down and filled with substandard furniture and insufficient numbers of books. Districts also had to deal with inadequate funding, which limited the amount they could pay teachers.

Despite the challenges, Oregon men and women still trained for the teaching profession and bravely traveled to new places in order to instruct young minds. One such woman was Ada Bell.

Teacher—Ada Bell

Ada Bell glanced anxiously about as the stagecoach pulled up to Bakeoven, Oregon. Sixteen-year-old Ada had borrowed the $4.00 she needed for the ticket to get there from The Dalles and thought someone was going to meet her in this freezing place. At an elevation of three-thousand feet, the cold winds coming off of Mount Hood sent temperatures in Bakeoven below freezing six months out of the year.

The town of Bakeoven sits in eastern Oregon, northeast of the Warm Springs Indian Reservation and nineteen miles east of Maupin as the crow flies. In 1897, it consisted of a hotel, a blacksmith shop, a store, a post office, a meeting hall, a stage stop, and a school. Ada Bell was its newest teacher. She remembers that first

Students in their classroom in the old Eola school in Eola, Polk County, Oregon. Their teacher stands in the rear of the room by the stove, ca 1930s—courtesy Salem Public Library

Stage station at Bakeoven, Oregon, in the 1870s—courtesy Oregon State Library

day: "I expected someone to meet me at Bakeoven. It was Saturday night, and supper time when we got there. No one was there to meet me. I was so frightened."

Ada eventually found her lodging and her schoolhouse, such as it was. Ada's first impression of Bakeoven had been something of a disappointment, and her first impression of the school wasn't much better. She described the spartan atmosphere with the words, "I had never once imagined myself teaching in a room like this one. Large rude desks, floor of rough wood, walls also of rough lumber, no paper, no ceiling, not one thing to brighten the dull effect."

While cleaning the schoolroom on the first day of class, Ada watched through the window as her seven students walked up the path. She was so young and inexperienced that she could only draw upon what she had heard other teachers do, greeting each of her students with, "Good morning."

Ada fought back her nervousness and disappointment at the reality of her first teaching job by focusing on the students before her. "I saw that it was best to be content," she wrote. "These pupils were not the ones of whom I had fondly dreamed, but they were humans with intelligent minds, and were placed in my charge. I thought of how much I should try to do all I could to improve their minds, and how I'd try to help them to learn and be happy."

The students were mostly the sons and daughters of German and Swiss homesteaders and shepherds who wished their children to become Americans. With a school term of just three months, there wasn't a great deal of time to teach. This limited time became even shorter as the children were occasionally absent from school to help with the farming or to take care of younger children.

Ada Bell taught school at Bakeoven, Oregon in the early 20th century—courtesy Ann Rosene and Binford & Mort Publishers

Teacher in primary class, Marion County, ca early 1900s—courtesy Oregon State Library

Ada returned for several more terms at Bakeoven. On July 4, 1901, she closed her school for the last time saying, "I shall always think lovingly of the place and people and my dear, dear pupils which almost seem to belong to me, I love them so."

Teaching During World War II—Naomi Van Dyke

Naomi Van Dyke wasn't a teacher. But in 1943, the Talent School District (near Medford, in southern Oregon) put out a desperate plea for teachers. Her husband was off fighting the war, so she decided to "help out." She began teaching the fourth grade, but transferred midyear to the high school to teach geography, economics, home economics, and U.S. history, as well as to supervise a study hall and tutor students who had transferred in and were trying to finish a course in a foreign language.

The trouble for Naomi was that she hadn't had a course in geography or home economics herself since the eighth grade. And just as the war had impacted Naomi's decision to teach, it also impacted her curriculum. Rationing limited the materials available for home economics classes, and these shortages often meant short lessons. The conflicts overseas changed borders and place names so quickly that teaching geography was no small feat. Naomi had to get material from the front page of the newspaper as often as from a textbook.

Cooking class at the Oregon School for the Deaf in 1952—courtesy Oregon State Archives

Banking

Banking was on the minds of Oregonians even before statehood. In June 1857, citizens voted to hold a constitutional convention which resulted in a constitution limiting public debt and placing tight controls on banks and corporations. Although it is likely that lending and borrowing was common between individual settlers and as part of running a business, banking as a stand-alone business was not a common activity in the early years of Oregon's statehood. Merchant William S. Ladd co-founded a bank in Portland in 1859, but no occupations specific to banking were listed separately in the 1860 census of Oregon.

However, more banks opened as the state grew. In addition to Ladd, two other successful Portland merchants—Henry W. Corbett and Josiah Failing—founded banks in Portland which became important to the city's economy. In 1867, Ladd joined with former *Oregon Statesman* newspaper owner Asahel Bush to co-found the Ladd and Bush Bank in Salem. By the early 1900s, banking was well developed in Oregon. In the 1910 census, Oregon counted 555 bankers and bank managers, of which sixteen were women.

Manager—Laverne Pritchard

One of the occupations not associated often with women in 1910 was bank manager. That didn't stop Laverne Pritchard. Laverne's grandfather, Joshua Mason, came to Oregon in 1853. He had been a casket maker (largely due to a diphtheria epidemic). That occupation didn't suit Laverne at all, so in 1909, at just twenty years old, she went to work for Citizens Bank on Grand Avenue in Portland (now U.S. Bank).

One day in 1910, Laverne's boss, the bank manager, came in with a golfing buddy who happened to be the branch manager for the Bank of California. Laverne could hardly believe the story that unfolded. The two had placed a bet on their golf game, and Laverne's boss had lost. What was the object of the bet? It was Laverne herself. It seemed her boss had been talking her up so much that the Bank of California manager had decided he wanted to hire her away. Laverne's boss objected, and the two made a wager that the winner of their game of golf would get to keep or hire her, and Laverne's boss lost.

It wasn't the most elegant way of finding a new job, but it turned out well for Laverne, who eventually became assistant manager.

Laverne Pritchard pictured in the 1930s—courtesy Margaret Pritchard

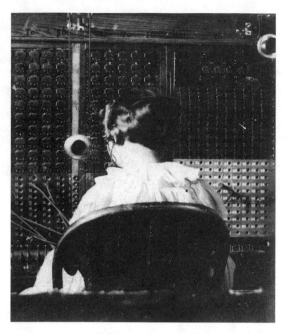

Telephone operator, Marion County, ca 1915—courtesy Oregon State Library

Since women managers were not at all common, Laverne used her initials to sign things: L.C. Pritchard. It's likely that Laverne worked mostly behind the scenes, communicating mostly by paperwork rather than in person. She had a great deal of authority, though, hiring and firing employees, and signing off on loans and payments of up to a million dollars. That was a lot of money, but Laverne herself didn't see much of it. Her salary of $125.00 a month provided a sufficient, but not extravagant, living.

What is perhaps one of Laverne's most unusual work stories involved the everyday task of counting money. Funds came into the branch in the form of gold coins. The tellers would put them in $100.00 stacks. They then counted the money in the short stack which was left over, which made it easy to tell how much money they had in their trays. Unfortunately, one of the tellers was a bit clumsy, and one day his stack of gold coins went flying, with some coins going down one of the heat registers in the floor. Everyone had to "heave to" and help count the spilled money, but no one ever knew if they'd recovered it all.

When the branch moved and they tore down the old building everyone wondered if they would find missing gold coins in the heat registers. They did not. It seemed that some quick-thinking individual had figured out a way to retrieve them unbeknownst to the others, because the registers were empty.

Laverne may not have found the missing gold, but her success in business inspired other women all the same. Her mother, Edna Hershner, was very proud of her daughter's accomplishments. After her daughter had been working at the Bank of California for about ten years, Edna decided to go into business for herself.

Edna saw an ad for a sheriff's sale of a cottage in Rockaway Beach (on the Oregon coast). Using "butter and egg" money she'd saved, Edna bought the place. Up until that time Edna had been a housewife, tending to cooking, cleaning, and caring for the children. Her husband, Frank, hadn't known she had an entrepreneurial spirit and wasn't too happy about it. Edna said that he never really accepted her business venture, but she didn't let that stop her; she wasn't about to give up her dream of being a property owner. Not only did she keep the cottage in Rockaway Beach—which she rented out—but in two year's time she'd also saved enough money to buy the duplex next door. Eventually she'd even earned enough to purchase an entire hotel. That twelve-unit hotel still stands to this day.

Edna Hershner pictured in 1939—courtesy Margaret Pritchard

Native Americans in the Early 1900s

Although it was not listed in the 1910 census and was rapidly declining in economic importance, the longest-standing occupation in Oregon can be characterized as "hunter-gatherer." Oregon's native population had inhabited the Pacific Northwest for more than ten thousand years, according to archaeologists. Oregon's native population was largely killed off by diseases brought by the European hunters, trappers, and settlers during their initial exploration of the region. By 1910, the census counted only 5,090 Native Americans in Oregon. Almost all of these were located in rural areas. Native Americans in Oregon were outnumbered by 7,363 Chinese, and were only a little more numerous than the 3,418 Japanese. The 1910 census listed those 5,090 people as belonging to ninety-four tribes with members in Oregon. Some of those tribes only had a single member, while the largest tribes—the Warm Springs and the Klamath—had over 500 members each.

Of those age ten or older, about 50 percent of Native American men and 7 percent of Native American women in Oregon were listed as gainful workers in 1910. (The definition of gainful workers excluded work around the home by women and children.) Most of those so listed worked in agriculture. Men in the Warm Springs and Klamath tribes were mostly farmers, farm laborers, and stock-raisers. Women in the Klamath tribe included some servants. In the Rogue River and Wasco tribes, men were usually farmers and farm laborers. The Umpqua tribe's male members were listed as farm laborers or "lumbermen, raftsmen, and woodchoppers." Umatilla tribe males were mostly farmers.

A Native American holds a large basket. Though unidentified, she is likely a member of the Northern Paiute Tribe. She is standing in front of the opening of the Alturas-Klamath Falls railroad cut-off in September, 1929—courtesy Oregon State Library

Transportation

The coming of a transcontinental railroad was anticipated as early as the 1850s. Railroads were expanding in Oregon in the late 1800s, a process greatly enhanced by the arrival of Oregon's first and second transcontinental railroad connections in 1883 and 1884. The transcontinental railroad's arrival boosted both trade and population. With a worker population in the neighborhood of twelve thousand, steam railroad laborer was one of the most common occupations among male workers, regardless of race. In 1910, the state had about two thousand five hundred miles of track, and this length

Mogul steam locomotive #3621, photographed somewhere in Eastern Oregon, probably in La Grande — courtesy Oregon State Library

was increasing by an average of more than one hundred miles per year. The railroad laborers spent long days building roadbeds, tunnels, and trestles, as well as laying crossties and tracks. Additional workers filled the jobs of locomotive engineers and firemen (men who stoked the fire to drive the engine), as well as brakemen and conductors.

In eastern Oregon, wheat farming became much more profitable once the railroads were able to carry the wheat to Portland. In Oregon's larger cities, workers unloaded grain from railcars at the ports to put it on ships bound for market. Workers were also employed in making grain sacks and farm implements, and in the various clerical and managerial jobs related to international trade.

Working the Rails — Haralambos Kambouris

Haralambos Kambouris was only twenty-two when he left his native Greece to come to America in 1912. The diary he kept between then and 1915 reveals the tough working conditions on the railroad line near Glendale, Oregon (between Roseburg and Grants Pass).

> Monday, October 8, 1913. In this work there are three groups working, one Greek, one Mexican, and one Arab. Our group and the Mexican changed the rails of the track and the Arabs who were loading the rails stopped working…The day was rainy and cold, we could not feel our hands because of the cold. We had been loading the rails for one hour. By bad fate a rail caught the left hand of my friend and partner Nicholas Boutsikos and fractured his two large fingers without anyone being aware of it… Inside the tunnel there was water and they wanted to replace the supports with new ones. It was dangerous for many reasons, and, also, very dirty and hard…out of the 30 in our gang only 15 would come to work. I and A. Douros were not absent from work at all.

Railroad track laying crew, ca 1930 — courtesy Oregon State Library

Groomsmen — James Smith

James Smith's first job in Oregon was at the John West Lumber Company in Clatsop County (read about John West on page 52). He married John's daughter Eva, and the pair moved to Portland, where his real career began.

Jim, as he was called, ran the stage for the Oregon Hotel, picking up hotel guests from the Portland Terminal Railroad Station, as well as from the docks along the Columbia River. Jim also made deliveries and hauled freight for the hotel. Jim would have had the responsibility of providing food and water for the horses, making sure their stalls and equipment were clean, tending to any minor wounds, and harnessing them up to his carriage whenever he needed to pick up guests, or to a wagon if he needed to go on a freight run.

James Smith sits atop his carriage, used to transport passengers from the train station in Portland—courtesy James Aalberg

Organizing Labor—The Creation of Unions in Oregon

One of the first unions in the Pacific Northwest, the Industrial Workers of the World (the IWW or "Wobblies," as they were nicknamed), came to Portland in 1907. This union was composed of unskilled, working-class laborers, including miners, loggers, and farmhands. The members of the union were known for their willingness to take militant action in order to achieve their goals.

During the recession that preceded World War I, employers in the lumber industry had used the poor economic conditions to their advantage in gaining control over the workforce. In 1917, as the demand for wood increased with the onset of the war, the IWW orchestrated a huge walkout among Oregon lumber workers, demanding higher pay and a shorter workweek. The strike was not successful. The federal government suppressed it after only a few months, and that, combined with the IWW's diminishing funds, sent the laborers back to their jobs.

As a continuation of their protest, however, workers deliberately decreased their output, producing only about 15 percent of the normal amount of wood. This prompted the federal Department of War to send Colonel Brice P. Disque to the region to investigate. The colonel immediately created two new organizations to break up the IWW's continued protest.

One of these groups was the Spruce Production Division (SPD), which was composed of some twenty-seven thousand enlisted men. The second group was the Loyal Legion of Loggers and Lumbermen (the "Four L"), which was essentially a federally sponsored labor union comprised of civilian workers. Those who joined the Four L were guaranteed an eight-hour workday and healthier working and living conditions in return for agreeing to be fully productive

Wayne Morse, 1900-1974

At age 30, Wayne Morse was dean of the University of Oregon School of Law. He successfully arbitrated a ferryboatman's labor dispute in 1935 and was appointed Pacific Coast arbitrator by the U.S. Secretary of Labor in 1939. He was popular with both employers and unions. In 1945 he became a U.S. senator. In 1946 he unsuccessfully opposed passage of the Taft-Hartley bill, which reduced the power of labor unions.

Wayne Morse—public domain photo

William U'Ren—courtesy Oregon Historical Society

workers who would not strike. Members of the IWW who joined the Four L thus in some ways received their original demands, though not in exactly the manner they had hoped. Unfortunately, getting what they wanted in the short term meant submitting to their employers, conceding all negotiating power, and forfeiting the advantage in the long term. Those who did not join the Four L ended up blacklisted by employers, who were suspicious of potential radicals or traitors. Overall, participation in the Four L peaked in 1918 with approximately 110,000 members. It declined thereafter until finally disbanding in 1938.

In 1929, the National Lumber Worker's Union (NLWU) formed. It favored the use of old IWW tactics and was openly sympathetic to communism, but the union was never able to bargain effectively with mill owners. It disbanded in 1935, and members were encouraged to join other unions.

In addition to the well-known, typical employer–employee labor disputes that occurred during the 1930s, there was also a great deal of conflict between different labor unions. For instance, the very large American Federation of Labor (AFL) decided in 1935 that it wanted to focus on recruiting and including only skilled craftsmen. Those who did not agree with this shift in the union's focus broke away from the AFL and began their own group, the Committee for Industrial Organization (or the CIO, which later changed its name to the Congress of Industrial Organizations).

Following this, employees at several of the large sawmills in the Portland area left the AFL and formed the International Woodworkers Association under the CIO. The employees who remained affiliated with the AFL then boycotted and picketed the mills, causing worker lockouts and shutdowns. The employers, along with Oregon Governor Charles H. Martin, sided with the AFL. The dispute raged for several years between different groups associated with either the AFL or the CIO. By 1939, however, the two unions were able to sign a temporary peace agreement while working on longer-lasting negotiations. In 1955, twenty years after the original split, the two unions finally came to an accord, reuniting to form the AFL-CIO.

The 1930s were a difficult time for unions and businesses alike; throughout Oregon and the Northwest there were several large labor strikes. The first notable one, in May of 1934, occurred all along the West Coast. Members of the International Longshoreman's Union (affiliated with the AFL) walked off their jobs.

Because the longshoremen were responsible for loading and unloading cargo ships, this strike effectively crippled shipping all along the coast. In many areas, striking workers used physical force to prevent strikebreakers from getting to job sites. In places this resulted in violence, including in Portland and Coos Bay. The violence, in turn, resulted in police intervention, although in Portland it took two months before they were willing to step in.

The striking longshoreman received a great deal of support from local communities, primarily among the working class. Despite the low availability of jobs and the high number of unemployed people, support was so strong that employers were able to fill only a few of the positions left vacant by striking workers.

Eventually, both sides of the conflict agreed to federal mediation of their demands. The longshoremen won extensive concessions, including higher pay, a thirty-hour workweek, and less arbitrary hiring practices.

A year later, in May of 1935, there was another huge strike in Oregon. An estimated thirty to forty thousand workers affiliated with the AFL's Sawmill and Timber Workers' Union (which is sometimes also called the Lumber and Sawmill Workers' Union, or LSW) walked off their jobs in mills, logging camps, and wood product factories. This shut down about half the mills in the Northwest, including most of the ones in the Portland area.

The striking workers tried using force to close some of the mills that remained open—those that could continue to operate with fewer workers or that were nonunion. This resulted in bitter and violent conflicts and forced local law enforcement to intervene in many of these disputes.

Unlike during the longshoremen's strike, there was limited local support for the lumber and sawmill workers. For instance, the *Oregonian* described the strike as "futile." The *Coos Bay Times* came out with a much stronger editorial against it, arguing that there was no way for business owners to meet union workers' demands in the strained economic conditions of the Great Depression and praising those workers who chose not to strike.

The strike finally ended in August of 1935 with some concessions to the union. Wages were raised from $0.45 an hour to $0.50 an hour, workers were given a forty-hour workweek, and the LSW union was officially recognized in logging and sawmill camps. All the same, these gains were far less than the union had hoped for, and some workers considered the strike a complete failure.

Some blamed the strike's failure on the International Brotherhood of Carpenters and Joiners, another union under the AFL, which had joined LSW in the strike. Members of the LSW argued that the Carpenters had conceded too soon. This rift continued, finally causing the disgruntled LSW workers to break away from the AFL in July of 1937 and create the International Woodworkers of America (IWA) under the CIO.

In 1936 and 1937, some of the longshoremen again went on strike. This strike was considerably smaller than their 1934 strike. The only noteworthy outcome was that the striking workers eventually broke away from the AFL to form the International Longshoremen and Warehousemen's Union under the rival CIO, fueling the already intense contention between the two. That year the National Labor Relations Act of 1935 also went into effect. Its goals were to protect rights on both sides (the rights of employers and of employees), to promote collective bargaining (the ability of workers to join together to negotiate with their employers, often in the form of unions), and to cut back those labor and management policies in the private sector that might harm workers' welfare (penalizing unfair labor practices).

While there were several large and bitter strikes during the 1930s, they were very likely made less severe by the presence of the New Deal programs (President Roosevelt's government programs to combat the Depression, including various reforms, emergency relief, work relief, and agricultural projects), which mandated a minimum wage on their projects and allowed for collective bargaining. The federal presence also provided a helpful mediator when local negotiations were stalled or otherwise ineffective, allowing disputes to be settled relatively quickly.

Gus Burnett—courtesy Tom Burnett and Joanne Broadhurst

Road Building

Gus Burnett

By the early 1900s, Oregon's population neared seven hundred thousand. No longer a sparsely inhabited wilderness, the state had large cities full of businesses, with stores and customers who needed good roads—the former for shipping goods, and the latter to get to those stores to buy those goods.

Back in the 1840s and '50s, Philip Foster hired crews of men to cut the Mount Hood Toll Road. Later he helped build Foster Road as a way to get from his farm in Eagle Creek to the Willamette River in Portland.

Up until the early part of the twentieth century, most roads were simple farm roads. As the automobile caught on, the need for better roads quickly emerged. As populations swelled, local governments needed men to build local roads in and between towns. In Clackamas County, the job of keeping track of that participation fell on the newly elected constable, Augustus "Gus" Burnett. Gus Burnett was the grandson of Philip Foster. See Philip's story on page 58.

Maude and Gus Burnett's wedding picture—courtesy Tom Burnett and Joanne Broadhurst

Back in those days, people could pay taxes by contributing time, or equipment, or both to road building. Gus kept an official record book in 1914 for Clackamas County Road District 43; it shows whether a man worked a half, a three-quarter, or a whole day, as well as whether he worked alone or with a team of horses.

The record book also gives clues as to the type of work these crews did. The activities included "Ditching," "Grading," "Hauling," "Spreading," "Rolling," "Corduroy," and "Culvert Repairing." "Grading" a road meant having a team of horses haul a specially made wagon with a large metal "scraper" attached to the bottom, so as to even the road out. Men using hand shovels would also come alongside to finish the job. Some Oregon roads (like Boones Ferry Road) were covered with gravel that was compacted using a steam-powered tractor with a roller on the front. "Spreading" could involve laying down stone, brick, gravel, or even concrete, though this last was very expensive. Paving with asphalt didn't come along until years later.

In 1904, there were exactly 141 miles of paved road in the United States. Most roads were either dirt or covered with gravel, sand, clay, shell, planks, or corduroy. "Corduroy" refers to placing logs perpendicular to the direction of the road to cross a muddy or swampy area—somewhat like a log bridge, but on the ground. It made for a bumpy ride, but at least buggies and cars didn't get stuck in the mud.

Gus The Farmer

Supervising road construction wasn't the only thing occupying Gus Burnett's time. In 1903, he purchased back one hundred acres of the original 640-acre Foster Farm out in Eagle Creek for $4,500.00. That's fifty times what Philip Foster spent on the entire land claim back in 1847.

Gus raised pigs on the farm. He drove a herd of pigs to market in Troutdale, traveling twenty miles through Gresham on Foster Road. In fact, he saved the money he bought the land with by raising pigs. Gus would always have at least one sow and nineteen or twenty piglets running around, along with some sheep and goats. Visitors to the house often found a piglet or small lamb behind the stove. If the animals' mothers rejected them, Gus would raise them inside until they could be on their own. Gus also grew prunes, hay, and corn.

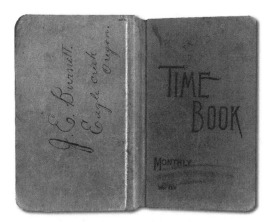

Gus Burnett's time book, in which he recorded time spent by workers building roads in Clackamas County— courtesy Tom Burnett

Goats on a hillside on Gus Burnett's farm in 1917—courtesy Tom Burnett

Oregonian—April 19, 1935

Vernonia Strike Voted for To-day: Clark & Wilson Loggers Act Unanimously

Employees of the Clark & Wilson Lumber Company voted unanimously to go on strike, reportedly spurred by recent firings of union workers who were replaced by non-union workers. The union leaders plan to meet with the employers. They argue that if negotiations fail and a strike occurs, it would be entirely the fault of the employers.

Steam Donkey in action, near Eugene, ca 1900—courtesy Oregon State Library

The Timber Industry

Between 1900 and 1910 there was a vast increase in the amount of timber cut from Oregon's forests. This occurred mainly along the Columbia River Basin. Jobs in the forest were difficult and dangerous. Teams of oxen were used until the beginning of twentieth century, when steam power entered the forest and steam donkeys helped pull logs up steep slopes. The man running the steam donkey was called a donkey puncher.

Life as a Logger

Loggers often worked in camps of two hundred men. A typical work schedule consisted of ten- to twelve-hour shifts six days a week. The work was not only tiring, but dangerous, with the ever-present potential for massive trees to fall and roll along the slopes.

Timber fallers near Silverton, ca 1900—courtesy Oregon Historical Society—Drake 351

The process of logging began with the fallers. Fallers used sharp axes to make wedge-shaped undercuts on the trunk of huge trees. They then sawed through the backside of the tree with manual saws, making sure the tree fell to the undercut side. Next, the loggers cut off the limbs and, when necessary, cut the log into shorter lengths. Finally, the loggers used giant sets of wheels pulled by a team of oxen—and later by horses—to lift one end of a log and drag it to a river or, when available, a railroad.

Logger operates saw, ca 1900 —courtesy Oregon State Library

Railroads caused rapid growth in the number of mills in Oregon, as they increased the ease of harvesting in many previously unreachable forests. The new mills were large and, during the early 1900s, several of them claimed to be the world's largest.

Loggers were not always single men who lived in the woods like trappers. Despite the deadly perils of logging, some men with families became loggers. Some, like Arthur Barber, had families who followed them to the logging camps.

Arthur Barber has his horse shod at a livery stable in Boring. Arthur is the one bending over the horse, ca 1907—courtesy Glenn Jones

Arthur Barber

Arthur settled in Boring, Oregon, around 1905. Like many people, Arthur had more than one profession. He was a logger, but he also spent time as a miner, barber, dentist, freight hauler, and bridge builder.

For the first few years in Boring, Arthur farmed land near the town while his children attended school. But farming didn't bring enough money for Arthur to support his family, so he took a job shoeing horses at the Boring Livery Stable. In 1910, Arthur took work as a logger at a camp in Diston, east of Cottage Grove. It was a rough life.

Working a Team of Horses — Mart Booth

The wagon wheels creaked and the horses snorted as Mart Booth fought to control them and avoid upsetting his cargo. Twelve years old was awfully young to be working, but the family needed him so he had to just buckle down and do it.

Mart began his career hauling lumber around Cove, Oregon, near the Wallowa Mountains of eastern Oregon—a career that would span the next sixty years of his life. Mart's dad, the Reverend

Mart Booth stands with his team of horses, ca 1917—courtesy Betty Stewart

By 1890, stationary steam "donkeys" with winches and steel cable were added to horse-drawn logging operations to help drag logs out of the woods. Steam tractors followed. In the early 1920s, gasoline- and diesel-driven Caterpillar tractors replaced horses as the power that pulled logs out of the forest. Chainsaws—developed in the 1920s—came into general use after World War II and further increased the output of loggers.

Mart Booth (on the right) poses for a photo in 1915—courtesy Betty Stewart

Luke Booth, had settled in Cove when there were only a few families there. (Read Luke's story on page 37.) Later, in 1903, Mart was part of a quickly growing timber industry.

Life in the woods matured Mart Booth quickly. The square-shouldered man with neatly trimmed hair only vaguely resembled the young man fighting his team of horses. Mart moved from Cove to Meacham, Oregon, nestled in a narrow mountain valley between Pendleton and La Grande. Though Meacham boasts some of the coldest temperatures on record for Oregon (negative fifty-four degrees Fahrenheit), that didn't stop Mart from venturing out into the woods. He dressed in a plaid shirt and suspended pants, his shoulders covered with a heavy mackinaw jacket and his feet protected by corked boots that were carefully oiled to keep his feet dry.

Mart learned to control his team of horses so well that he found work skidding logs (the term for pulling them out from where they fell) even when jobs were scarce. Mart was known for his honesty and willingness to work hard. His lifelong love of horses spurred him to leave home one day in the 1920s with his shiny new Model T Ford and come home with a handsome pair of matched black horses. While out, he'd decided that he liked horses better, so the Model T had to go.

Working at the Mill—Alfred Woodward

The Brower sawmill east of Portland wasn't the world's largest, but it was big enough to give Alfred Woodward a good job. Near the turn of the twentieth century, he worked as something called an "edgerman." The edger had six saws. Alfred worked the edger to turn boards into sizes and shapes that were marketable. Running the edger took great skill, and Alfred's abilities on the job were rewarded with a position as the head sawyer.

The head sawyer managed all the saws in the mill, laid out logs, and signaled the setter (the person who judged the logs to make sure each one was cut to the best advantage). Alfred did well in this position, and was later promoted to foreman. Alfred passed down a description of how a logging and sawmill operation worked in the early 1900s.

> Pairs of fallers used an axe and a crosscut saw. Sawyers cut the trunk into logs. The skid road extended two miles into the forest. A team of twelve to fourteen oxen hauled the trains of logs. At Bridal Veil Lumber company,

Fir-Tex Board Plant in Portland, ca 1930s—courtesy Oregon State Library a donkey engine used cable and tackle to move the logs. The logs were dumped into a pond where the pond man moved the logs into reach of the mill. The lumber was put down the chute into the flume. Then the lumber was wheeled to the Latourell planing mill for finishing. Some Douglas-fir lumber was made into fine flooring. Lumber was wheeled to the dry kiln, then shipped on the Columbia River, and later on the railroad. All the work was done by hand including the construction of roads and logging railroad trestles.

If the name Latourell sounds familiar, that's because the mill was founded by Joe Latourell, whose story you read on page 29.

Alfred Woodward around 1900 with Columbia River Loggers—courtesy Shirley Schwartz

Retail Trade

Retail stores were a feature of Oregon life almost from the beginning. In 1860, Oregon had 446 merchants and nine storekeepers. By the late 1800s, Portland was a place where shopping and entertainment establishments could be found on all major thoroughfares. By 1915, Morrison Street had become the home of major department stores such as Meier & Frank, as well as many specialty stores. The 1910 census counted more than 9,000 salesmen and saleswomen and more than 3,800 clerks in Oregon's stores. Of these, one-quarter were women. There were also 1,400 deliverymen for stores. Another 10,400 people—almost all men—worked as retail dealers. Portland, with a population of 207,214 people in 1910, was a center of retail trade. But stores were also a part of life in Salem, Astoria, Eugene, Medford, and other less populous cities.

Storekeeper—John F. Lawrence

John F. Lawrence sat quietly on the train as it approached the station in Medford. This small southern Oregon town's population was only 8,849, but it was growing rapidly thanks to a new industry—growing pears. The Lawrence family had heard Medford was a wonderful place to live, so they were coming from Minnesota by train with all their belongings. They had also heard about the pears. John's daughter Ruth once wrote a letter about how wonderful those pears were to eat.

After the train slowed to a stop, John stood, his grip firm on the case he'd carried on his lap all the way from St. Paul. John was a watchmaker, and as a watchmaker, he needed tools to make a living.

OREGON STATESMAN— SEPTEMBER 5, 1945

Crowds Swamp Salem Stores

A "phenomenal" business day was reported by several merchants Tuesday who said that crowds swamped their stores during the day and bought merchandise in every available line.

John F. Lawrence at his workbench around 1940—courtesy Ann Horton

John ushered his family off the train and retrieved another important piece of cargo from among the luggage—a workbench. Now all John needed was a place to set up shop.

John opened his store on South Central Avenue, sharing quarters with the Southern Oregon Electric Company. Since he needed more to offer than just making and repairing watches if he wanted to keep his business going, he purchased the inventory of a local jeweler who was quitting and leaving town. John paid $500.00 for the merchandise and began a business that is still going strong one hundred years later.

After a fire destroyed the first building, John moved his store to another, which he shared with a ladies' hat shop. John continued quietly building his business, expanding his inventory to include diamonds. The work of a jeweler takes concentration and fine motor skills. John possessed both. He also possessed one more thing: a little pipe that he enjoyed smoking. He turned even that into a tool, blowing through it to fan little flames in the pipe bowl, which he would use to solder pieces of metal together.

Open a Store, Start a Town—Charles Tigard

Wilson Tigard settled in the area just south of Portland, near the Tualatin River, around 1853. Wilson didn't have the money to buy the land, but the people already living there were so anxious to have others move in that one family lent him two oxen. He used those oxen to buy a large piece of property. He then paid off the loan by cutting and selling timber from the land he'd purchased.

Wilson's son, Charles, decided to open a little store on the property, at the corner of McDonald Street and a little dirt road that would eventually become Oregon Highway 99W. Getting the mail delivered was not an automatic thing in the 1880s,

Inside John F. Lawrence's store prior to 1911—courtesy Ann Horton

John F. Lawrence Emporium, ca 1916—courtesy Ann Horton

and Charles had to volunteer to be the postmaster for two years—without pay—to persuade the Postal Service to deliver to the area.

The Postal Service named the place Tigardville after Charles Tigard. When the railroad arrived in 1907, the name had to be shortened to Tigard because railroad employees kept delivering freight bound for Wilsonville, a bit further to the south. Apparently the names Wilsonville and Tigardville were too similar.

Charles took in bundles of mail arriving by rail and distributed them to individual boxes. No one had mail delivered right to their door; they had to come into the store to retrieve it. This was part of Charles's business model—if people had to walk through his store to get the mail, they might also see something to purchase as they walked the aisles toward their mailboxes.

Sales at the store did well enough, but were not great. So around 1916, Charles decided he needed other markets to sell his goods. He began growing and canning vegetables, and raising rabbits and chickens. Every Saturday morning Charles loaded up his horse and buggy and traveled down Taylor's Ferry Road (at the time, it led to a real ferry) to Macadam Avenue and into Portland. Charles rented a stall at the Yamhill Market, which stood in the area between Second Avenue and Fifth Avenue. Today, the Portland Farmer's Market sits just a block from where the Yamhill Market stood then.

First Paper Route—Curtis Tigard

While Charles Tigard hauled vegetables to the market in Portland, his son Curtis came along for the ride. At only seven years old, Curtis was already becoming an entrepreneur, selling *Oregon Journal* newspapers for $0.03 a copy.

Curtis would approach customers in and around the market. "The good corners were all taken," he remembers, "I started avoiding them after getting chased off once or twice." Curtis didn't have any special cry such as, "read all about it." Instead, he just asked people if they needed a newspaper.

As for profit, Curtis purchased his newspapers for $0.02 cents each and sold them for $0.03, so he made a penny a paper. He remembers sticking the money in his pocket and saving up for something called a Liberty Steak. "It was a glorified hamburger without the bun," Curtis remembers.

Money management became a more important part of Curtis's life in the 1950s when he served as a bank manager. (Read the rest of his story on page 147.)

Wilson and Mary Ann Tigard pose for a picture sometime in the mid to late 1800s—courtesy David Tigard

Charles Tigard sits on the porch of his Tigard home—courtesy David Tigard

Curtis Tigard is about to feed his dog on the porch of the Tigard home. This was taken around the time Curtis sold newspapers on the street corners of Portland—courtesy David Tigard

Fishing for the Family—Charles Thompson

Charles Thompson loved to fish. Around the turn of the twentieth century, Charles and a neighbor would take an annual trip from Hood River to the headwaters of the Deschutes River in central Oregon to fish.

They would make camp and for the first six days, they used hooks with no barbs on them. The fish they caught they simply threw back into the river. Then on the seventh day, a wagon full of ice would arrive at their camp. Charles and crew would then fish their hearts out for the entire day, throwing the fish into the back of the wagon. In one day, they would catch enough fish to feed two families for an entire year.

When the state limited the number of fish you could catch in a day to one hundred, Charles seriously questioned whether he should even go out fishing anymore, though it clearly didn't stop him altogether.

We know all this in part because of a benefit Charles received in 1928—a lifetime fishing and hunting permit, given to Oregon pioneers. It says, "This certifies that C.D. Thompson is entitled to hunt game birds and animals and to angle in conformity with the law." Fishing wasn't Charles's only love. He also owned one of the first cars in Hood River. That privilege also brought a new type of chore—changing flat tires.

Charles Thompson changes the tire on his 1909 Apperson Jackrabbit— courtesy Alice Mullaly

Job Hunting

Clergy, Salesman, Postal Worker—Arthur Gardner

His dream job kept eluding him, but that didn't keep Arther Gardner from seeking work and satisfaction wherever he could find it. Arthur was the grandson-in-law of William Hunt Wilson, who came to Oregon with Jesse Applegate in the 1840s. (Read William's story on page 26.)

Arthur worked as a minister, and even appears in a 1928 listing of ministers who worked in Oregon. At one church he was offered a salary of $600.00 per year. This was about the wage a general laborer would earn. Arthur struggled at times to make ends meet, so he began to explore other occupations to help supplement his income and support his growing family.

We're fortunate that Arthur kept a detailed record of his search for work and for a career. In this record, we can see what it was

The diaries of Arthur Gardner— courtesy Christy Van Heukelem

really like for someone going through the trials and tribulations of various kinds of work at the turn of the twentieth century.

In June of 1902 Arthur resigned as pastor of the Canby and Turner congregations and moved his family back to Drain (where he and his wife had lived as newlyweds). He wrote, "Now that I have more time to devote to it, I am studying more diligently on my course with the Columbian Correspondence College for the Observer (Weather Bureau) examination."

The Weather Bureau had only existed as a civilian organization for twelve years at the time (it had been a military organization before) and was a part of the U.S. Department of Agriculture. The idea of forecasting the weather was still a relatively new one. Official three-day weather forecasts hadn't begun until 1901, a year prior to Arthur's interest. The post office delivered forecasts with the daily mail. The only problem was that while the mail went out at 7:00 AM, the forecast for that day wasn't completed until 10:00 AM, so the mail carriers actually delivered the forecast from the previous evening.

Arthur applied for the civil service examination on September 20, 1902, even though the test wasn't given until October 21 in Portland. The application process was so difficult that Arthur needed two other men to help him. Meanwhile, he continued to study meteorology. In the months that followed, Arthur begins to record daily weather observations in his journal, likely as practice for becoming an official weather observer.

While waiting to take the exam, Arthur worked selling books. On October 9, 1902, he "canvassed" a series of books called *Self & Sex*, written by Dr. Wood-Allen, the World Superintendent of the Purity Department for the Women's Christian Temperance Union. That job didn't pan out well. He wrote, "On this date I set out to canvas Salem with the *Self & Sex* Series, but after a few days work, gave it up as a bad job. I sold about twenty-five books there all told."

After taking the exam, while he waited to hear back on the results, Arthur went through several jobs. At one point, he stocked shelves at Ransom & Sons grocery store for half a day. Shortly after that, he performed a funeral. It was an unusual funeral for two reasons—not only was it, in his words, the "rainiest" funeral he had ever attended, but even more unusually, he got paid. He wrote, "Today I had a new experience. Mrs. Wood sent me $2.00 to pay me for my services at the funeral. Of course it was not asked for nor expected."

Arthur Gardner portrait during his days as a minister—courtesy Christy Van Heukelem

The Gardner family sits on the front porch of their home in Drain. Pictured are Arthur Gardner, his children Eb, Esther, and Doris, and his wife May—courtesy Christy Van Heukelem

Despite receiving payment for the funeral and for occasional work in the store, doubts about his path in life continued to plague Arthur. On his birthday, he wrote, "December 21. I am 29 years of age on this date. It hardly seems possible that I am so well along in years—and have accomplished so little. I hope my 30th year may be fruitful of some definite and lasting work taken up."

As 1903 began, Arthur received some hopeful news. Friends writing on his behalf had convinced John H. Mitchell, one of Oregon's U.S. Senators, to help secure a position for Arthur in the Weather Bureau. During the next several months, Arthur's journal entries start with weather observations. However, despite his practice, and the influence of a U.S. Senator, Arthur never got the position. He noted in early 1904 that his eligibility had expired.

In January of 1903 Arthur accepted a position from J.A. Black to work in his store and post office. He also notes that he caught chickens to sell. After a few months, J.A. Black sold the store to Moses Mack. In May of 1903, Moses gave Arthur a raise to $1.50 a day. Unfortunately, just four days later, a layoff notice overshadowed the good news.

Undaunted, Arthur went to tallying lumber work for the Palmer Lumber Company. He received $1.75 a day and was promised $2.00 a day once he had learned the job. He didn't note it, but the mill job only lasted until July, when Arthur went back to work in a store as assistant postmaster. In 1904, he took a job as a substitute mail carrier for the Portland Post Office.

Arthur purchased a mail carrier uniform for $1.50 and began to learn various routes around Portland including Sunnyside, Portland Heights, and Albina. He wrote about delivering mail in the rain and when it was one hundred degrees in the shade. One day in particular he noted delivering forty-three *Ladies' Home Journal* magazines. His schedule fluctuated between eight and a half and well over ten hours a day, depending on how much mail he had to deliver and the difficulty of the route.

His job subbing for the post office ended on October 10, so Arthur turned to yet another job, selling life insurance for the Germania Life Insurance Company of New York and later for Mutual Life. After a few months with few sales, Arthur started looking for work once again.

November found Arthur "rustling" for jobs by answering help wanted ads. He mentioned being "hard pressed for lack of cash" and once again tried selling books door-to-door. This time he sold "Chase's Last Complete Work Receipt Book" and had some prospects, but few orders.

By the end of the month, his wife's parents had to send them money to help out. Arthur tried to apply for a conductor's job on the railroad, but found that they were not accepting applications. Next, he applied at a planing mill (which produced finished lumber) and at Olds, Wortman & King department store, one of the oldest companies in the Pacific Northwest (the former building of which today houses the Western Culinary Institute).

Salem Postal workers in 1894—courtesy Oregon State Library

Things started to get desperate for Arthur. His bookselling was going nowhere. His former boss offered him a position back at the store in Drain, but he didn't accept, writing, "I can't afford to do that. Must become regular letter carrier."

In December, Arthur was finally hired at the Portland Iron Works Foundry for $2.00 a day. It was a job of desperation and not one Arthur liked at all. "I worked in the moulding room—foundry. It is not easy, very smoky and dirty work. It will be 'till I can do better… I don't like foundry work, but can endure it for a time. It is very dirty and pretty heavy at times."

Arthur once again subbed for the post office in early 1906. Finally, in May, he received word of a permanent appointment as a letter carrier. He was sworn in as a regular letter carrier on May 14 and began delivering mail the next day to the Highland neighborhood along Route 44. He wrote, "I have an easy route. Like it very well." Apparently, it was a little too easy. Arthur noted that the superintendent "thinks I am getting along too easy, I think," and so added two more streets to his route.

It appears that Arthur earned $83.60 every other week for delivering the mail. His routes weren't always easy. He wrote of being bitten by dogs on September 7 and 11, 1906, and also recorded being "swamped" with Christmas package deliveries on December 29 and 30 of that year.

Arthur and May Gardner later in life—courtesy Christy Van Heukelem

His journal for 1906 concludes with one final entry "December 31: Cloudy, Lt. rain at night. May is much better. I make one trip with a great load."

Arthur Gardner worked hard to care and provide for his family—whether as a pastor, salesman, grocery clerk, mill worker, foundry worker, mailman or some combination thereof—for much of his life. No doubt, he also helped carry that burden for his daughter Doris and her husband, Chester Corry. Doris and Chester had to live with the Gardners in the early 1930s when the Great Depression had thrown Chester out of work (read about Chester on page 105).

The Great Depression

Oregon farmers fared poorly in the 1920s because of an agricultural depression and drought. These problems meant fewer jobs on the farm. Oregon sawmills also employed fewer people. So even though the Great Depression didn't get started until October 29, 1929, with the stock market crash, Oregonians were feeling the effects of a downturn well beforehand. When the market crashed, it fell more than 12 percent in one day. The economic chain reaction that followed was a disaster. Banks failed in droves, causing foreclosures of homes, farms, and businesses. The collapse of business meant fewer jobs to put food on the table, and the loss of savings meant no financial cushion through the hard times.

Herbert Hoover was president of the United States at the time. He was the first and only president from Oregon, having spent his boyhood in Newberg and some time as a young man in Salem. Hoover felt that local communities and states should provide relief during the Depression, rather than the Federal government, and so even as late as 1932, only 1.5 percent of all U.S. government funds were being spent on relief efforts, averaging about $1.67 per person.

During the Great Depression, Oregon's timber industry declined. The production of sawlogs fell from a pre-Depression peak of 4.5 billion board feet in 1929 to only 1.5 billion in 1932. The number of jobs in the industry declined almost as steeply, leaving many workers hunting for jobs elsewhere.

Nationwide, about one in three non-farm workers had no job. In 1930 between 64,000 and 120,000 Oregonians were without jobs. Compared to the early years of the twenty-first century, when between 100,000 and 115,000 people found themselves unemployed

Worker picking hops in the 1930s
—courtesy Oregon State Library

in any given month, those Depression numbers don't seem so alarming. But in 1930, Oregon's population was less than 1 million, while in 2000 the population was roughly 3.5 million.

When Franklin Roosevelt took office in 1933, he instituted a broad range of public programs to put people back to work, programs collectively known as the New Deal. One, the Beer Act of March 1933 (which effectively put an end to Prohibition) meant that hop-growers could again employ pickers in the Willamette Valley. It also meant that brewers like Blitz-Weinhard could once again resume production. The day after Prohibition ended, a small winery opened its doors in Salem. The Honeywood became well known for wine and brandy and still operates today. Read more about the Oregon wine industry on page 136.

One of the most important ways that the government helped put people back to work was to create immense public works projects. The Works Progress Administration (WPA), which was created for the purpose of getting unemployed workers (in fields ranging from manual labor to the fine and performing arts) back to work, undertook many such projects.

One such project was Bonneville Dam, built by the Army Corps of Engineers between 1933 and 1937. The project employed four thousand people for years. The dam resulted in the availability of inexpensive electric power. Almost immediately, jobs in aluminum plants opened up. Demand for aluminum grew rapidly in the airplane-manufacturing industry during World War II. The U.S. government built and operated four new aluminum plants in the Pacific Northwest, selling them after the war to private companies.

Roosevelt's administration also helped create the Civilian Conservation Corps (CCC), a sort of peacetime army to fight the erosion of the country's national resources. The CCC provided employment for millions of American men, including Chester Corry.

Landscape Architect—Chester Corry

Chester Corry rarely took "no" for an answer. The Great Depression had hurt employment chances for millions, but Chet, as he was called, remained undaunted. First, he and his wife, Doris Gardner, moved in with her parents in Portland. (Doris's father, Arthur Gardner, is featured on page 100.) Wearing his new suit and a new pair of shoes, the purchase of which left him only $5.00 in pocket money, Chet earned a job at Lambert Gardens.

New Deal Projects in Oregon

Bonneville Dam

Oregon Folklore Project

Timberline Lodge

Numerous federal buildings

Post offices

Canby City Hall

Oregon State Capitol & Library

Klamath Falls Armory

Corvallis High School

Oregon School for the Blind dormitory

Medford Sewage Disposal Plant

Major coastal bridges

Source: Oregon Bluebook

Worker on transmission lines at Bonneville Dam—courtesy Oregon State Library

Charles McNary—public domain photo

Chet and Doris moved to the Laurelhurst area while Chet worked at Lambert. His job was to draw plans and design the color of plantings for the gardens there, using skills he'd acquired as a landscape architecture major at Oregon State University. But after three years, there was simply no money to pay Chet. He quit, and the couple moved back in with the Gardners. Times were hard; one month, he made only $15.00. Out of work and desperate, he finally got a job with the city of Portland designing planting plans.

Chet joined other landscape architects as part of a WPA project. But even this lasted only so long:

> I took all kinds of work along the gardening line. At one home, I was told to come to the back door for my money as all the other help did. Well, they were poor pay and this did not last long. I had purchased an old car and we drove it all over Portland looking for jobs. All the big landscape offices were not doing anything either. What a mess I was in. All of us, in fact.

Chet's former boss at Lambert suggested he try getting a job with the National Park Service. After a recommendation from Mr. Lambert, Chet went to work at Mount Lassen Volcanic National Park in northern California.

Chet worked with a crew of twenty World War I veterans planting flowers along roads through the new park. It was tough work, but Chet appreciated the great food, fresh air, and good company in his camp.

In his free time, Chet started experimenting in a test garden. He would find plants in the evenings and then plant them in his garden. He had to convince a truck driver to help him haul water to his fledgling garden, but his experiments taught him valuable lessons he would soon employ up north in Oregon.

On a trip home from California, Chet stopped in Ashland to check on an assistant park supervisor's job and never left. This job involved building a park in a mostly undeveloped canyon, which was difficult work. The good news was that the same man who had created Golden Gate Park in the San Francisco Bay Area had planned this one. The bad news was that this was the height of the Great Depression, which meant no money and no staff. According to Chet, "at that time you'd fall in love with anything that spelled work."

Chet did everything from cleaning the restrooms to pouring hot water into an old Ford dump truck—which required a crowbar to keep it held together—and cranking it to get it started in the morning. However, Chet not only held that dump truck together, he held the entire park together, and began scouring the watershed of Mount Ashland for young, three-foot-tall trees to plant in the park. Soon, incense cedars, pinion pine, weeping spruce, and high bush cranberry were thriving in the mile-long city park. Chet once again got some help from the WPA. "We had lots of fun," Chet said about putting in water systems and planting roses, as well as building waterfalls, rapids, bridges, a nursery, a playground, and even a zoo.

One time, some workers dropped a young cedar. Its root ball "exploded." Chet simply picked up the young tree, stuck it in a bucket of water, and planted it anyway. It later became one of the largest trees in the park. Circumstances may not have been ideal, but by struggling through and continuing despite them, good things were able to grow.

Chester Corry in Lithia Park—courtesy Christy Van Heukelem

Helping the Unemployed

National relief programs were vital during the 1930s, but local programs played a large role as well. Two important Oregon institutions were started during the Great Depression: employment services and unemployment insurance. The year 1933 saw the birth of the national re-employment service. Offices were set up around Oregon to find people willing to work on public works projects such as the Bonneville Dam and large highway projects.

Then in 1935, the state of Oregon passed an unemployment compensation law. This created an agency, the Unemployment Compensation Commission (UCC), which found work for those able. When the UCC couldn't find them work, they paid them a small weekly amount to tide them over until they could find a job. To pay for this, employers paid into a fund based on their payroll.

The first unemployment insurance check was issued to James H. Allen on January 15, 1938, in the amount of $15.00. That year, the Commission handled 96,741 new claims, took in $6.1 million from employers, and paid out $5.9 million in claims.

Despite the massive public works programs, Oregon and the rest of the United States didn't emerge from the Great Depression until the start of World War II.

Workers wait in line to file for unemployment, ca 1960s—courtesy Oregon Employment Department

World War II

The year 1941 marked a distinct change for work in Oregon. The United States was thrust into World War II, and the transition from peace to war had a profound effect on the workplace.

That year many Oregon workers enlisted in the military to serve in World War II. In 1942, four thousand Japanese-Americans were sent to internment camps. Only about half returned to the state after the war. Many Japanese lost property and jobs during their internment. A 1948 law was designed to compensate for some of those losses, but paid out only $37 million on $148 million in claims. The law did not compensate for lost wages at all. In 1988, the Civil Liberties Act compensated each person interned with $20,000.00. Subsequent studies have found that this was far short of their actual losses.

The war created a severe need for shipyard workers as many young men left their stateside jobs for positions in the military. Advertisements everywhere proclaimed "We Need You" in the shipyards.

Jobs Open Doors for Minorities

Kaiser Shipyards—which operated the Portland-Vancouver yards—recruited workers from across the country. They needed skilled workers. During the war nearly two hundred thousand people moved to Oregon seeking stable work in beautiful surroundings. Portland's African-American population grew by tenfold during the war years. But success wasn't easy. When they arrived, African-Americans typically found obstacles to overcome, such as difficulty

Charlotte Bail installs a light fixture on a Liberty ship being constructed at the Oregon shipyard on December 27, 1942—courtesy Oregon Historical Society—OrHi36982

Kyotaro Chikuo and wife, Tatsuyo on the front steps of their home in Independence. The Chikuo's operated a hop farm in 1936. They were likely taken to internment camps in 1942 and lost everything—courtesy Oregon State Library

Chikuo hop yard's campground store with patrons—courtesy Oregon State Library

getting into the labor unions because of racial discrimination. Many had to settle for lower-skill jobs. Nevertheless, many stayed in Oregon, and the state's minority population rose between 1940 and 1960. Of course, despite this growth, the minority population was still only 2 percent of the total population—a far smaller share than that of the Pacific states as a whole, where they were almost 9 percent, or that of the United States as a whole, which had a minority population of about 12 percent.

Women Working During the War

During the early 1900s—and especially during the Depression—women had more difficulty getting jobs than men because men were given priority. During the war years, the number of jobs related to the war effort—including shipyard jobs—increased significantly, as did the length of the average workweek for individual workers doing those jobs. The U.S. government saw both the opportunity and the need to recruit women to meet the demand for workers. With rising prices and the rationing of food and other necessities, many women also needed the money to help their families—it wasn't just patriotism that drove them to the shipyards.

Women of all ages—from their teens to their fifties—worked in the shipyards. At one point in 1944, there were forty thousand women on the job at Portland-Vancouver, nearly one-third of the area's shipyard workers. Many worked as welders, while others worked as electricians, painters, crane operators, or machinists. Typical wages were $1.20 per hour for both women and men, a good wage at the time.

Work was done on all shifts, around the clock. Much of the work involved welding, grinding, and polishing. It was noisy, dirty work. At the end of a shift, the workers often had rust all over their clothes and in their hair. Getting on the bus afterward could be embarrassing. And yet they found some of the work, such as welding, very satisfying, and even artistically beautiful. They also found a sense of pride in having helped produce the ships.

Although many men accepted women as coworkers, others resisted this new arrangement and made the women feel uncomfortable and unwelcome. In some work environments, there wasn't any sign of discrimination or sexism, while in others, supervisors made advances on women. Some women felt they had to do their jobs a little bit better than the men in order to be accepted.

Two maintenance carpenters hang a sign at Willamette Iron and Steel on September 6, 1942, indicating that work will continue on vital war projects even on the Labor Day Holiday—courtesy Oregon Historical Society—OrHi90403

Iona Murphy—welder for Oregon Shipbuilding Corporation, ca 1943–1944—courtesy Oregon Historical Society—OrHi56117

A group of women workers at Commercial Iron Works discuss issues with a counselor at lunch in March of 1943—courtesy Oregon Historical Society—ba007561

Women worked seven days a week for twenty or thirty weeks at a time. Working at the shipyards and still being responsible for the traditional duties of a wife and mother was a difficult task for many. Kaiser Shipyards added a food service that made it more convenient to buy and bring home ready-made dinners. Kaiser also built two twenty-four–hour child-care facilities toward the end of the war.

What was it like working in one of those shipyards? Fortunately, we have a daily account from a woman assigned to learn what it was like to work as a welder on U.S. Navy warships.

Augusta Clawson—Shipyard Diary of a Woman Welder

"I have completed six days of training, and tonight am the proud owner of two things: one—a black metal lunchbox complete with thermos; two—a firm conviction that I shall become a welder." Augusta Clawson's initials were stenciled in white paint on that black metal lunch box. She sat, holding an apple in her hand, next to a black welder's helmet, also stenciled with the initials AHC.

It was 1944, and Augusta was part of a cause and a movement. The cause was helping to defend America by building warships in Portland's Swan Island shipyards during World War II. The movement was of women into the workforce, a necessity in wartime, and a permanent change in the makeup of work in Oregon and across America.

Augusta actually worked for the U.S. Office of Education. She was sent to the shipyards as an investigative agent because there was a high turnover problem in the yards. Women were needed for all

Augusta Clawson worked at a Portland shipyard as a welder during World War II. She went through the training to find out why women weren't sticking with the job for very long—courtesy Smithsonian Institution

kinds of jobs during the war, including welding giant ships together, but too many left after training. It was Augusta's job to take the training, do the work, and try to discover why women didn't stay in those jobs.

She kept a daily diary of her time working for the Oregon Shipbuilding Corporation at Swan Island in Portland, one of seven shipbuilding yards created by Henry Kaiser. During the war, the U.S. Employment Office put up big signs with such slogans as "INDUSTRIAL WOMEN: Shipyard Women." Augusta applied for a welder job and was told training would take forty to sixty days.

Transitioning from weaving to welding was difficult for Augusta. She noted during her training days that "It gets hotter than mustard under those heavy leathers. The tight band of the helmet makes your temples so sore that it even hurts to touch them when you're away from the Yard. The gloves make your hands sweat. The arcs (arc welders) give off fumes, and lots of us have burns. But no one kicks. They all take what comes in their stride…"

The work was not the only difficult thing about the job; the environment she worked in was also taxing. "There is nothing in the training to prepare you for the excruciating noise you get down in the ship. Any who were not heart and soul determined to stick it out would fade out right away. Any whose nerves were too sensitive couldn't take it."

Augusta learned quickly, and soon spouted welding jargon like an old pro, talking about "chipping slag" (knocking off leftover welding material) and "tacking butterflies" (tacks are small welds that hold an item in place for the final application of the welding material). Clambering around on a half-built ship could be dangerous. Here's her description of part of a day climbing around the ship she was constructing:

Liberty Ship William Clark launches from Portland shipyards on October 26, 1941—courtesy Oregon Historical Society—OrHi36102

OREGON JOURNAL—
MARCH 4, 1939

Chinese Pickets Withdraw as Port Officers Promise to Accept No More Scrap

The Chinese residents in Astoria ceased picketing the Japanese freighter Norway Maru after the Astoria Port Commission agreed to no longer accept scrap metal bound for shipment to Japan. The Waterfront Employers Association had threatened several days earlier to close the port unless the Chinese ceased picketing, which would have shut down most of the plants in Astoria and nearby towns. Local employers thus added their voices to the pleas to cease the pickets. The picketers remained reluctant to do so until the shipment cessation order was issued by the port authority.

Pipefitters and sweepers from Commercial Iron Works pose for a group shot on June 13, 1943—courtesy Oregon Historical Society—OrHi64476

I was assigned to do production-welding on the poop deck… Five weeks ago I'd have cold shivers, for it meant easing over the edge of the deck and lowering myself from the top scaffolding to another about five feet below. As there was nothing to hang on to en route, this meant that my landing aim had to be good or I might start a rapid descent between ship and scaffoldings down to the street far below. However, my imagination held good. I swing by it, set my eyebrow at the prescribed angle, and prepared to tack a dog just above—when my hood skidded down without ceremony and I couldn't see a thing. It's a weird feeling to be suspended somewhere between heaven and earth and suddenly have all vision blotted out; it does queer things to your sense of balance. You grope out cautiously for fear of making a quick move in the wrong direction, and sometimes the ship seems to slide just out of reach with deliberate orneriness.

How did Augusta find the relations between men and women workers in the yards? She told one story of a man named Pat who treated women like they couldn't handle the difficulties of being a shipfitter. One day Pat offered to give Augusta a "rest" and told her she should go home. Another time she laments about a man named Bill and the fact that "…he never smiles, never indicates that he is satisfied with what you do, and never lifts a finger to help." Upon Augusta's return from a week off in Cincinnati, a man she called Colorado at first acted mad as he read his paper at the breakfast counter. After a pause he said, "Well, you know, it was…lonesome here."

Augusta's job, though, was to figure out why women quit soon after completing training. She told plant managers that the mere eight days of training that most women were receiving were inadequate for anyone completely unfamiliar with the concept of welding. The problem wasn't that the women weren't capable of doing the work, but that they needed a firm hold on the skills necessary to do it. Augusta wrote, "I have stated it before—what exhausts the woman welder is not the work, nor the heat, nor the demands upon physical strength. It is the apprehension that arises from inadequate skill and consequent lack of confidence."

Though we don't know whether the shipyard heeded her suggestion for better training, Augusta observed another problem faced by women working during the war: child care.

In 1942, Congress passed the Lanham Act, which provided funds to build child-care centers in cities most affected by war production.

When Kaiser Shipyards' management announced a million-dollar nursery, however, none of the women workers liked the idea. Mothers were concerned about mixing their children with others who might be a bad influence. They also voiced concerns about proper diets for their kids.

Management explained that the center would be staffed with a doctor and nurses, would provide excellent care, and that it would not be "a charity thing." The women finally relented, remembers Augusta, saying, "Maybe that nursery is a good thing." By 1945, the centers around America had served six hundred thousand children, making them the "largest commitment to public childcare in American history."

Conclusion—After the War

Following the war, Oregon's soldiers returned home. They found the workplace at home quite different from the one they had left behind. There were many more women and minorities in the workforce, and the availability of jobs had changed. The economy, boosted by wartime spending, provided many new jobs, as well as the opportunity for disposable income and savings—a radical change from the down times of the Great Depression and the uncertainties of a world at war.

Many of these returning soldiers, with a new sense of security, settled down and started families. The economic trends begun in the '40s and '50s, plus the coming baby boomers (those children born after the war), would radically change the nature of work in the last half of the twentieth century.

Times were definitely changing, and opportunities becoming available. Four war veterans decided to take advantage of this new atmosphere and go into business together. They didn't know exactly what they'd sell, but one of them, Howard Vollum, had wanted to make something called an oscilloscope (an instrument that temporarily shows fluctuating electrical quantity variations as a visible wave form). This relatively new invention was becoming an important instrument in the growing field of electronics.

In the spring of 1946, Howard had created a portable oscilloscope, and the fledgling company had its first product. They named the company Tektronix and helped establish Oregon's high-tech industry. Tektronix eventually became Oregon's largest private employer.

Howard Vollum, 1913–1986

Mr. Vollum co-founded Tektronix with Jack Murdock in 1946. He served as president of Tektronix (Tek) for many years. The company helped provide the foundation for Oregon's high-tech industry and was the precursor of many companies in Oregon such as Mentor Graphics, TriQuint Semiconductor, and Planar. Tek's employment peaked in the early 1980s at around 24,000. Although Tek's employment declined to about 4,400 in 2007, Oregon's high technology industry as a whole provided more than 50,000 jobs, many of them paying high salaries. Read more about the Tektronix story on page 149.

Howard Vollum—co-founder of Tektronix—courtesy Tektronix

Workers assemble transformers, cathode ray tubes, and resistors on the factory floor at the Sunset Tektronix plant in Beaverton, unknown date—courtesy Tektronix

Section Three

1950–2009

Introduction

In the half-light of dawn, only the low growl of a truck motor broke the silence of the forest. Elmer Harris Taylor worked the gears as he willed his truck up steep dirt roads deeper into the hills of Linn County. Pat Brown sat across the cab. Their conversation turned to how they planned to attack the giant Douglas fir they'd had their eyes on. Cutting it down would be hard enough, but how would they ever wrestle it onto a log truck and get it to the mill?

Elmer needed that tree to come down. As a graduate student at a seminary in the 1950s, he was more used to studying Greek than figuring out how to fell a tree. But that tree, harvested from his land, could go a long way to making sure he had enough money to return to school in the fall and complete his studies. Did he succeed? Read Elmer's story on page 122.

Elmer Harris Taylor worked at the beginning of a quickly changing period in the history of work in Oregon. Many jobs Oregonians perform today bear little resemblance to those they performed in this period of relative prosperity and calm.

Rapid Changes in the Second Half of the Twentieth Century

Many aspects of work in Oregon have changed in the years from 1950 to today. The state's population more than doubled, growing faster than that of the rest of the nation. The number of employed people in Oregon tripled, and the number of unemployed more

Job seekers looking for work in the 1960s—courtesy Oregon Employment Department

Oregon Then and Now—Annual Averages[1]		
	1950	2007
Population(1)	1,521,341	3,745,455
Labor force	654,800	1,927,802
Employed	607,500	1,827,285
Unemployed	46,600	100,517
Unemployment rate	7.1%	5.2%
Workers in labor–management disputes	700	100
(1) Census (1950) and Portland State University (2007)		

than doubled. Women greatly increased their presence in the paid labor force, especially in office, professional, and service occupations. Their addition caused the workforce to grow substantially faster than the total population.

As elsewhere in the United States, unionization declined, and labor management disputes—such as strikes or lockouts—are a less prominent part of the economy today than they were in or before 1950. Self-employment is more common, aided by the trend toward professional services and the development of personal computers and telecommunications technology. Today, for instance, an accountant using a phone and a computer with accounting software can operate his own business, rather than having to work with large mainframe computers in an office with many other workers, as would have been the case shortly after 1950. (See how computers and technology have affected the office on page 151.)

Automation has become a bigger part of the workplace, first with electricity powered machinery and then with personal computers and information technology. The quantity of information available to the average worker has increased dramatically due to the expansion of scientific research and publishing, and new telecommunications technologies. Many occupations relying heavily on manual labor have lost much of their importance in the economy due to automation, particularly with regard to employment numbers.

Government regulation plays a greater role at work than it did earlier in the twentieth century. Starting with the Civil Rights Act of 1964, laws added a minimum wage, outlawed many forms of

A job seeker waits in line to look for work, downtown Portland, ca 1960s—courtesy Oregon Employment Department

Top Occupations in 1950			
1	Clerks, stenographers, typists, and secretaries	42,655	7%
2	Farmers and farm managers	40,145	7%
3	Non-farm laborers	39,537	6%
4	Salesmen and sales clerks	36,708	6%
5	Farm laborers and foremen	29,942	5%
6	Wholesale and retail trade buyers and managers	28,000	5%
7	Truck and tractor drivers	19,758	3%
8	Mechanics and repairmen	18,782	3%
9	Lumbermen, raftsmen, and wood choppers	18,756	3%
10	Carpenters and cabinetmakers	16,412	3%
11	Teachers, college professors, and librarians	14,602	2%
12	Private household workers	10,808	2%

1961 Average Cost of Consumer Goods

Bluebrook Margarine, per Pound
$0.15

Boy's Life Magazine, Monthly
$0.25

Chap-et Lip Balm
$0.35

Chrysler Newport Automobile
$2,964.00

Daisey BB Gun
$12.98

Ethan Allen Desk, Four-Drawer
$85.60

Flintstones Child's Feeding Set
$1.99

Kelvinator Air Conditioner
$169.00

Kodak Brownie Super 27 Camera
$22.00

Kraft Miracle Whip Salad Dressing, Quart
$0.43

Magnavox Broadway Stereo Theater
$495.00

Magna-Lite Shop Light
$6.95

Pioneer Ebonettes Kitchen Gloves
$0.98

RCA Victor Tape Recorder, Reel-to-Reel
$99.95

Scott Tissues, Two Packages of 400
$0.39

Scripto Goldenglo Lighter
$5.00

Tums Antacid, per Roll
$0.12

Ultra-Sheer Seamless Stockings, Box of Six
$5.28

---

workplace discrimination, provided for more worker safety, and mandated leave for employees with special circumstances, such as maternity. (See more detail on this later in this section.)

International trade became a bigger part of Oregonian's lives. A common label on cheap imports used to read "Made in Japan." Today, Japan is one of the world's largest economies, and the products we import from there are mostly popular and high-quality. Today, China is the main source of cheap goods. Reduced trade barriers, expanding industrialization, fewer government regulations, and a massive labor force have allowed China to produce goods very inexpensively.

By the early 2000s, many consumer products purchased by Oregonians were made in foreign countries, especially China, and the United States was running a large trade deficit. People outside of the United States now sell us products and services once produced or performed only within our borders.

After the North American Free Trade Agreement (NAFTA) took effect in 1994, many U.S. companies opened factories in Mexico. As NAFTA effectively eliminated most of the trade barriers between Canada, the United States, and Mexico, it became highly profitable for U.S. companies to outsource jobs due to the availability of cheap labor in Mexico. Outsourcing has become a major part of business beyond our borders. Companies in India build large call centers to provide customer support all around the world at all hours, on a wide variety of products. Though America still exports machinery and many agricultural products, when it comes to consumer products, the normal procedure is for companies in the United States to develop ideas for products that are then produced by companies or subsidiaries abroad and shipped back to the United States for purchase by Americans.

The Postwar Years

Following World War II, Oregon's economy still relied mainly on natural resources, especially timber and agriculture. However, the war changed many aspects of life for working families in Oregon. Soldiers returned home from the war to work. They received educations thanks to the GI Bill (education grants afforded returning veterans). Jobs for teachers and professors increased in availability as America's baby boom generation—the large numbers of children born following the war—entered elementary school.

Students walking outside an unknown school, ca 1965—courtesy state of Oregon Archives Division

Teaching

In 1950, there were over fourteen thousand teachers in Oregon, reflecting large increases in the population of school-aged children. This increase led local school districts to ask taxpayers to fund the construction of new schools. However, Oregon's teachers had more than just new schools and new students to adjust to; they had a new war.

World War II was over, but a new war had begun—the Cold War with the Soviet Union. It began after the Russians successfully detonated a nuclear bomb in August of 1949. In 1951, Congress created the Federal Civil Defense Administration (FCDA), charged with helping communities protect themselves. Public schools quickly became centers for education and preparation for possible attacks on the United States.

Schools began conducting air-raid drills, where students practiced ducking under their desks as a protection against flying or falling debris during an air raid. The words "duck and cover" became commonplace as children prepared for nuclear attacks.

Education was becoming much more important. In 1930, only about one-third of the population had graduated from high school. In 1950, that statistic had jumped to over 50 percent. Increasingly, the goal of the public education system was to train students for higher education, as the job market demanded more technical and specialized knowledge—especially in the growing fields of information and services.

Brookings Teacher in 1953—Frances Morris

Most of all, Frances Morris recalls the principal. The head of the elementary school where she taught in Brookings would stand in the doorway to his office, plucking caps off little boys' heads and picking out those who were misbehaving in the hall. "He was always there and on time," she remembers.

Frances herself had a difficult time arriving to work on time. She had to get five family members off to school and work each morning—fed breakfast and sent off with lunch, as there was no cafeteria at the school—and still arrive at the school herself before 7:00 AM. This was her only alone time before students arrived. She didn't even have a key at first, until a sympathetic teacher lent her one and told her to make a duplicate. It was an early start, but it was also a short day. Administrators divided the school day into shifts because of a school policy against splitting up families. Frances benefited from this policy when the principal gave her the morning shift.

By the time Frances was ready to dismiss her students, the afternoon shift teacher was waiting outside the door, wanting some preparation time herself. Frances felt this was much better than the previous system, which required teaching from 7:30 in the morning until 5:30 in the afternoon with no breaks.

Even with teachers working in shifts, things at the school were busy. The student population grew so rapidly that there simply weren't enough teachers to go around. The shortage became evident to Frances when cold temperatures inside school buildings led many teachers to become ill. "So many teachers were sick and so few substitutes available in those days, that I, with a 'cough, cough, cough' situation on my hands, thought that if one more teacher stayed out, they would have to close the school."

Frances taught about sixty children in her class. For Frances, activities such as music, physical education, class photos, inoculations, and "weigh-ins" were unwanted interruptions to instruction in much more important subjects. "But no matter what came up," she says, "we insisted that the first part of the day should be for uninterrupted reading classes."

Alice Mullaly—photo taken by Tom Fuller

Teacher—Alice Mullaly

You might say that education is in Alice Mullaly's blood. An uncle of her grandmother, John W. Johnson, was the first president of the University of Oregon. Her grandfather, Charles Thompson, taught at Oregon State College (which became Oregon State University) and was the superintendent of schools in Hood River until 1915 (read Charles's fishing story on page 100). And her father, Charles Claude Thompson, served on the board of the Jackson County Parent-Teacher Organization.

Is it any wonder that Alice became a teacher herself? From the mid-1960s until 2008, she taught mathematics at schools and universities in southern Oregon. Alice has a good perspective on just how much teaching has changed over the decades:

> There is a lot more expected from schools from what used to be parental roles. Counseling and guidance is part of every teacher's workload now, and it didn't used to be. Nutrition, feed them—breakfasts, and lunches—and after-school programs because there is no one at home. Schools are expected to pick up all that.

The result, according to Alice, is that since teachers have only so much time and energy in a given day, the more time they must spend fulfilling parental roles, the less time and energy they have to teach. Still, there are plenty of rewards for today's teacher:

> Being in front of kids and dealing with students is by far the most rewarding part of teaching, because they are so alive and interesting and interested in so many things. When you can take a student who is terrified of math and turn them around into a future teacher who's excited to teach math, it is the best feeling in the world.

For Alice, grading papers is the most time-consuming and difficult part of teaching. These days she teaches only two classes at Southern Oregon University. She also does a fair amount of substitute teaching, which she says is great because she doesn't have to spend a lot of time on lesson plans—she simply shows up and teaches math.

The Timber Industry—Feast & Famine

During the 1940s, timber companies boosted manufacturing capacity to support the war effort, but in 1949 a manufacturing slowdown cut eight thousand jobs from logging and sawmills and sent the unemployment rate up. The industry replaced most of the lost jobs in 1950 and reached an all-time peak number of jobs in 1951. However, that was far from the end of the industry's rollercoaster ride over the hills and through the valleys of economic trends, interest rates, and housing demands.

Oregon had as many as seventy thousand jobs in logging and sawmills in 1951, as former military men and women gained access to affordable mortgages and postwar demand for housing surged. However, the number of timber jobs dropped to only thirty-nine thousand a decade later, as automation improved efficiency and the postwar surge diminished. As market demands shifted, companies

1961 Average Per Capita Consumer Spending Nationwide

Food	$462.19
Housing	$278.73
Auto Usage	$207.41
Clothing	$125.21
Recreation	$103.98
Utilities	$76.21
New Auto Purchase	$65.87
Personal Business	$65.87
Gas and Oil	$65.33
Tobacco	$38.65
Personal Care	$33.21
Physicians	$32.12
Religion/Welfare Activities	$29.94
Furniture	$26.13
Telephone and Telegraph	$26.13
Private Education and Research	$22.32
Auto Parts	$14.15
Dentists	$11.43
Health Insurance	$10.89
Local Transportation	$10.89

added more that seventy plywood mills between 1940 and 1960. Employment in Oregon's veneer and plywood industry grew from about five thousand three hundred jobs in 1947 to almost twenty-eight thousand in 1966 as plywood became the preferred building material for many applications. Jobs in particleboard and paper mills also increased.

Jobs in the Forest

Logging attracts workers able and willing to rise before dawn, commute to the worksite, and work at a physically demanding job in a wide variety of weather conditions. Working in the woods can be enjoyable, especially for those not interested in sedentary indoor jobs. Timber industry jobs include forest road construction, logging, and loading and trucking logs to mills. At the mills, workers unload the logs, operate sawing machines, and drive forklifts to stack the sawed lumber. Increasingly, the work has become automated. Loggers rely more on GPS (Global Positioning Systems) and satellite imaging to guide their activities. Millworkers use computer-controlled sawing machines. Just during the 1980s, automation cut the number of workers required to process a given quantity of timber by almost one-quarter. Additional automation has occurred since then.

Cutting trees and hauling them out of the forest is still hard work, despite all the automation. One man who can appreciate that is Elmer Harris Taylor, who logged his own land back in the 1950s.

Elmer Harris Taylor—Logger

Off Tum Tum Road in rural Benton County, south of the Marys River, a road wanders up through Scheele Creek to the timber claim of George Henry Harris (read George's story on page 71). Though he acquired it sometime before 1900, George never did much with that land beyond build a small cabin and scratch out a garden so he could claim it. Years later, it provided a living for George's grandson, Elmer Harris Taylor.

In the 1950s Elmer was finishing his studies at the Dallas Theological Seminary. He needed money to pay for school and to make ends meet, so he spent his summers cutting timber. Elmer had to figure out a way to harvest the timber from his land, so in 1951 he bought a big Ford F6 truck to haul logs out of the forest. He paid only $2,599.90 to buy it from Wilson Motors in Corvallis, using money he borrowed from his uncle.

Elmer's day began at daylight. He hired Pat Brown to help him wield a big two-man chainsaw to fell the monster trees on the property. "It was all brute strength and awkwardness," Elmer says. "We rolled them with a dozer blade onto cheese blocks that would hold the log in place. Then we would use a bulldozer sometimes called a par roller to get them onto the truck and haul them to Linn Plywood or Lebanon Plywood."

Elmer remembers one time when he and Pat looked up at a tree that was seven feet wide at its base. "We can take that down," he remembers telling Pat. But it wasn't easy:

Elmer as a recent OSU graduate in 1951—courtesy Elmer Harris Taylor

> The problem was we only had a five-foot bar on the chain saw. We got the undercut in, and then got in about eighteen inches with the chain saw and hit a pitch pocket. Pitch by the gallons poured down the shaft of this big Douglas fir. We pumped straight diesel fuel to keep the chain from freezing up. It took us three hours to bring that tree down. It was so big I had to build a road to haul it out. I got sixteen thousand board feet in that one tree.

In the ten weeks of summer, Elmer made enough money to support himself the rest of the year. "It was hard work. Good work. I only have a few scars to show for it." Just in the summer of 1959, Elmer harvested sixty thousand board feet of timber.

Forest land logged by Elmer in the 1950s—courtesy Starker Forests

Forest Management in the Twenty-First Century—Scott Hayes

Scott Hayes and his wife, Marjorie, stand next to a Douglas fir tree. Scott wraps a tape measure around the trunk at just the right height to determine how many board feet of timber the young tree contains.

Scott spent his entire career helping owners of small plots of land plant trees and protect them from insects and disease. But he never had the opportunity to practice what he preached until he retired from the Oregon Department of State Forestry in 2005.

Scott and Marjorie Hayes calculate the board feet in a Douglas fir on their property in northwest Oregon—photo taken by Tom Fuller

Now on his own forty acres, Scott can manage a model, sustainable forest of mature and younger Douglas fir, along with some cedar and madrone. Scott spends his days driving a small tractor around the steep property outside Forest Grove. He took classes in how to fell trees using one of his four chainsaws. Once he cuts a tree, he uses the winch on his tractor to haul it to a place where it can be picked up by a truck and taken to the mill.

Scott says they produce about two truckloads of timber each year. That's five to six thousand board feet. At that pace, Scott says, they could harvest his land forever. He buys and plants two to three hundred trees a year, each of them one foot tall, with a foot of root each. Scott spends most of his time grading the trees and thinning out the poor-quality ones as they grow.

Scott doesn't live on the land settled by his ancestors back in 1865, but he's only about thirty miles away from where his great-great-grandfather Thomas Hayes settled. And even the land he now owns was part of the Timmerman homestead of 1888. It's a pretty remote life, but Scott says there was just something about the land that lured him here and gave him a desire to manage it for his nephews. Scott plans to pass on the knowledge of how to grade a Douglas fir to them, just as his father passed on a love of the forest to him.

Wood Products

Oregon is known for wood products made from its large Douglas fir, hemlock, and ponderosa pine trees. Wood-product manufacturing grew rapidly in the first half of the 1900s but dropped back during the '60s. Then it rose again in the booming years of the '70s. It tumbled in the severe recession of the early 1980s, then again rose in the late 1980s. During the early 1990s, the reduction in timber harvests from federal forest lands—related to the protection of the northern spotted owl—reduced timber industry employment to half-century lows.

Floyd Hayes as a flume walker near Sheridan in 1920—courtesy Scott Hayes

Pilot Rock Mill in Pilot Rock, Oregon, ca 1959—courtesy Betty Stewart

EUGENE REGISTER-GUARD—
AUGUST 1, 1975

JOURNEYPERSON instrument TECH-
NICIAN wanted for permanent main-
tenance assignment in Pulp and
Paper manufacturing operation.
Union scale and liberal benefits.
Papermill experience desired. Inter-
ested applications [*sic*] male and fe-
male send resume to R.J. Manning,
American Can Company, Post Office
Box 215, Halsey, Oregon 97345. An
Equal Opportunity Employer. Male/
Female.

As the industry weathered its ups and downs, the mix of activities shifted as well. In the 1950s, logging and sawmill jobs dominated
the timber industry in Oregon, but these jobs declined rapidly as
veneer and plywood jobs expanded. By 2000, employment in logging and sawmills was outnumbered by jobs in veneer and plywood
and other wood product manufacturing. Rapid growth in veneer
and plywood jobs in the 1950s and '60s reversed in the 1970s as ori-
ented strandboard (a new plywood-like product made from wood
chips glued together under pressure) from the southeastern United
States invaded plywood's niche.

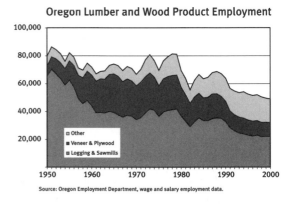

Oregon Lumber and Wood Product Employment

Source: Oregon Employment Department, wage and salary employment data.

Vickie Slack Fullmer—Loader Operator

During the 1950s, jobs in the timber and wood-products industry were
plentiful. As a little girl during this time, Vickie Slack watched with
great interest as her father, Lavern, drove his homemade tractor around
the family garden in western Polk County near the little mill town of
Willamina in the foothills of the timber-laden coastal mountains.

Lavern Carl Slack built that tractor from parts and pieces. Even
as a young girl, Vickie shared her father's interest in building and
operating machines. And she wanted more than anything to have a
chance to get behind the wheel herself.

Vickie didn't get to drive her dad's tractor then, but years later,
when it came time for Vickie to go to work, she used her interest in
machines and tractors to do what most women did not do—drive a
huge log-loading tractor around a veneer mill.

Vern's tractor with Vickie standing and
her sister Andrea driving—courtesy
Vickie Fullmer and Andrea Slack
Mobley

Lavern "Vern" and Retha Slack—courtesy Vickie Slack Fullmer and Andrea Slack Mobley.

Vickie comes from a long line of Oregonians who worked in the timber industry. Her maternal great-grandfather, Charlie Orsborn, worked seasonally in the woods in Valsetz, Oregon, in the early 1900s. Vickie's father, Vern, who was called "Red" in the woods, worked as what was known as a "highclimber" in the 1950s.

Highclimbers were the rare breed of loggers who took their lives into their hands by climbing trees hundreds of feet up to prepare them for felling. His work took him to the Tillamook area, Garibaldi, Estacada, and other places in the Coast Range. Vickie on her father:

> He was always positive and happy. Always had a great smile and sense of humor. He loved the woods and loved a challenge. He was a "can do" man, whether it was breaking a horse that no one else could break or highclimbing a tree. He was well-known for both. When no one else had the courage to do it, my dad would strap on his climbing gear and go for it! One of his mottos of bravado we often heard was "When it gets too rough for the rest of 'em, it's just right for a SLACK!" This was always followed by a huge grin and a twinkle in his eye. We know the story of the time that a few guys tried to climb this particular tree. One by one as they gave up and came back down, the foreman yelled, "Go get Red!" Dad took a lot of pride in his skill and bravery. He certainly had earned the right to crow a little. One time he climbed on up and sat on the top of the tree after topping it—and as it swayed back and forth, he ate his lunch just to show off. No wonder then, that as I was growing up, he taught me that anything I wanted to do, I could do it!"

Vern Slack "carries" a giant log, ca 1955–1960—courtesy Polk County Museum

When it came time for Vickie to work for the Boise Cascade Veneer Mill in Willamina, she was ready for anything. In the 1970s, mills like this were more or less segregated. The men "worked out back" in the yard with the loaders, and the women worked the "green chain" inside—sorting the veneer as it was peeled into thin sheets, cut into different sizes, stacked and banded, and then shipped off to plywood mills to be glued into sheets of plywood.

In the 1990s, however, things were changing. Women like Vickie began to make it known that they were perfectly qualified to run the same equipment as the men. That changed everything and gave Vickie her chance to be a tractor driver. Little did she know that her tractor would be so huge. Just the tires on the leviathan rose far above her height of five feet nine inches. She got her chance behind the wheel, not of her father's garden tractor, but of an L-120 Loader.

Vickie Slack Fullmer stands by her L-120 in 1995—courtesy Vickie Slack Fullmer

Vickie's job was to pick up logs that had been cut into eight-foot long blocks and ready them to be turned into veneer. One after another, she had to use the grippers to quickly grab a full load of blocks from the saw bins and place them into steam vats, and almost simultaneously unload the other vats of steamed blocks and put them up for the lathes to peel. Vickie on her job:

> To me it was just the fact that I had the courage to get on it and take that responsibility. The L-120 kept the whole mill running. It took a certain kind of determination to learn to run this machine. It was a very stressful job, since the whole production of the mill was dependent on the L-120 driver to keep the heated blocks fed into two high-speed lathes. As I drove that machine night after night—back and forth and around and around at a dizzying pace—I couldn't help but think back to my upbringing and how my dad had unknowingly prepared me to take advantage of this great opportunity. It was very rewarding for me.

Vickie's foreman told her she had learned to drive the L-120 faster than any other woman who had tried it. That was no surprise to Vickie, who had started imagining great feats of her own as a little girl watching her daddy drive his homemade tractor around the garden. "I just thought, 'If only my dad could see me now.' He would have been so proud and would have gotten the biggest kick out of seeing his baby girl, 'Tizzy,' on that huge piece of machinery."

Allen Stewart—In the Mill Office

Allen Stewart wasn't going to cut logs or stack lumber, but the owners of the Pilot Rock Lumber Company weren't about to let their new office manager hole up with figures and reports without seeing firsthand what cutting and stacking was like. So in 1951 Allen spent a few weeks in the mill, located in the small town of Pilot Rock—about fifteen miles south of Pendleton in northeastern Oregon. Allen lived about fifteen miles from the mill with his family, including his wife, Betty, whose grandfather, Luke Booth, settled in Cove, Oregon in 1865 (Luke's story is on page 37), and whose father, Mart Booth, worked hauling logs out of the woods with his team of horses in the early 1900s. (Mart's story is on page 95.)

Allen Stewart in the mid 1950s—courtesy Betty Stewart

After his time in the mill getting to know the operation, Allen oversaw the entire payroll for Pilot Rock Lumber, including vacation calculations. In the 1950s there were no electronic calculators or computers on each desk. Allen used an electric adding machine to do the payroll math. He made $300.00 a month when he started, and received a raise of $25.00 a month each year.

Work started when Allen left home around 7:00 each morning to pick up the company mail at the post office and carpool to the mill with fellow employees. He would make it home around 5:30 or 6:00 each evening.

Farming

Farming in the second half of the twentieth century was far more complex than in previous eras. Agricultural technology—both mechanical and chemical—changed rapidly and increased farm productivity. Self-propelled combines and circular irrigation systems were two types of mechanical advances. Chemical herbicides, insecticides, and fertilizers became widely used. However, many farmers—especially those on smaller farms—either couldn't afford the new technology or didn't want it. The number of farms in Oregon actually fell by 43 percent between 1945 and 1982 while the average farm size rose by 60 percent. Farming became big business, and farmers sold much more of their produce to out-of-state or even foreign customers.

Some smaller farmers got the best of both worlds, keeping away from automation (because they couldn't afford it) but still running efficiently (because they were resourceful). If they didn't have something, they invented it. A case in point: Austin Warner.

Farm buildings probably near Woodburn in 1950—courtesy Oregon State Library

Farmer/Inventor—Austin Carl Warner

When you're a farmer, the land gives but demands payment. Austin Carl Warner knows this well. Austin was born in the same house as his mother and his grandfather—the house built by his great-grandfather Wilson Carl, who worked hard enough as a carpenter to purchase 575 acres of prime farmland north of McMinnville. (Read Wilson Carl's story on page 21.)

Helping with farm chores started young and early for Austin. When he was six years old, his father, Austin W. Warner, began teaching him to drive a tractor. For much of his life, he rose at 4:00 or 4:30 in the morning to milk the cows, come in for some breakfast, and head back outside to clean the barn. Then it was on to the fields to drive his tractor, with which he would disk (run metal disks through a field to smooth the soil for planting), plow, and harrow (break up clods in the soil) fields of oats, corn, wheat, barley, and grass seed.

Austin attended a two-room schoolhouse not too far from the farm. Most days he would walk, but sometimes he would ride his horse. After school, it was back for more chores until the sun went down.

Don't get the idea that Austin disliked this work. It was just what was expected. It was what his dad, granddad, and great-granddad had done each and every day. Austin didn't shirk hard work, but he did always try to find ways to do more with less effort.

Austin W. Warner inherited the farm from *his* father, and in 1924 purchased St. Mawes Lad Marie, a very special Jersey cow that formed the foundations of the Willow Springs Jersey Farm. Feeding and milking are, of course, at the heart of running any dairy, and improving those processes had a dramatic effect on the farm. Austin Carl Warner remembers several innovations that he and his father implemented in the 1940s and '50s, innovations that made news at the time but might be taken for granted today.

The first problem Austin faced was getting harvested hay from the wagon into the barn. At the time, it usually took three or four people using hayforks to heave the hay into the mow (the part of the barn where hay was stored). Austin and his father figured out a less labor-intensive method. They used an old car transmission to hook up a gear reduction motor to the hay wagon. The transmission turned a metal draper, like a conveyor belt, which then blew the hay or alfalfa up into the mow.

Two generations of Austin Warners pose behind their tractor, ca 1940s—courtesy Austin Warner

Austin Warner works the fields of the Carl farm, ca 1950s—courtesy Austin Warner

Austin Warner works the device he helped invent to bring hay into the mow with less effort—courtesy Austin Warner

Sally, Tim, and Sue—the ideal cows of the 1950s—stand in their stalls on the Willow Springs Jersey Farm—courtesy Austin Warner

Father and son devised the system, obtained the parts, had others fabricated at a local equipment company, and then set up the first-of-its-kind hay blower. The invention got them a mention in the local newspaper and the *Interstate Tractor Farmer News:*

> Mr. Warner blows the chopped alfalfa into his barn, makes it easy for one man to handle the whole operation if necessary. The harvest is handled speedily, labor costs hit rock bottom and the crop is brought in with minimum of handling. Result: Maximum feeding from the hay crop at lowest possible cost.

Not content with just finding a faster way to bring the hay into the barn, the two Austins also tested an experimental technology that cured the hay more quickly. After reading up on techniques practiced on the East Coast, the pair devised a system of fans that blew air across the hay to dry it faster. It cost them about $500.00 to create the system, and about $1.00 a day to operate. The result was nothing less than fantastic. The new method allowed the two Austins to put the hay into the barn almost immediately after cutting, and to cure it more quickly than drying it in the field would allow.

The invention garnered praise for the Willow Springs Jersey Farm in the *McMinnville Telephone Register*, as well as a chance to have a special demonstration put on for area farmers by the county agricultural agent.

The dairy's innovative methods and prize-winning stock got a lot of attention outside of Oregon as well. The family's 1960 journal mentions that people from Idaho and Arizona paid visits to inspect the cows and bulls. But Austin Carl and his father weren't satisfied yet.

Milking the cows by hand was hard work that was neither efficient nor sanitary. In the 1950s Austin Carl and his father began installing automated milking machines and piping the milk straight from the cows into holding tanks and then into trucks for transport. They didn't invent these machines, but they were among the first to use them. By the latter part of the 1960s, they could milk a herd of ninety cows in just over two hours. The feat got them mentioned once again in the local newspaper as a "Grade A" dairy.

In 1970, the Willow Springs Jersey Farm attained the status of Century Farm—an honor bestowed by the state's Department of Agriculture and the Oregon Historical Society for farms that have been in continuous ownership and operation for over a hundred years.

At the time, Austin Carl Warner was asked if he ever considered slowing down the innovations. He replied, "You'd kind of think that after having a dairy farm in the family for one hundred years you'd have it made, but you find yourself constantly making changes to update the system."

Today, Austin still lives on the farm his great-grandfather bought in 1862. He leaves the farming to others these days, but he can still look out on the lush land that he's worked his entire life. "If I was younger I would still be out there," he says. It's easy to imagine him still waking before the sun and heading out to think of another innovation to make the farm run more smoothly.

Austin Warner stands on the Wilson Carl farm, in front of the home where generations of Carls and Warners were born—photo taken by Tom Fuller

Farm Labor

During World War II, Congress passed legislation to alleviate the U.S. labor shortage by encouraging Mexican workers to work on American farms. About fifteen thousand Mexicans worked in Oregon's agricultural sector. The program ended in 1964. Some of the guest workers stayed in Oregon and moved their families here from Mexico. Today, Hispanics make up 10 percent of Oregon's population and work in every occupation and industry.

Agricultural products were in strong demand after the war, as the population grew rapidly in the United States and war-torn countries needed food. Many native Oregonians remember working in agriculture as youths in the 1960s and '70s. Picking berries was a common job. In the following decades, migrant labor was used more extensively to tend and harvest crops, and the practice of hiring young people to help during the summer became much less common. As technology advanced and rising minimum wages made youth and migrant labor more expensive, farmers employed more machinery and shifted crops toward less labor-intensive species.

Nursery and greenhouse crops were some of the fastest growing segments of agriculture and became the top job-providing segments as well. In 2007, Oregon's nursery and floriculture production provided an annual average of 12,540 jobs. Fruit and nut tree farms employed about 7,650 people, the next-largest number of farm jobs, although the number of jobs in this part of agriculture varies dramatically by season. In total, recent estimates indicate Oregon's farms provide between 45,000 and 80,000 jobs, depending on the season.

Many people know Oregon as the Christmas tree capital of the world. A lesser known fact is that Oregon grows 98 percent of all

OREGON STATESMAN—
AUGUST 1, 1965

BEAN pickers wanted— Fred Heinz bean yard. Beginning second picking Monday, August 2. No transportation furnished. 5883 Angle Dr. 364-2444

A young girl picks strawberries from an Oregon field in 1958—courtesy Oregon State Archives

EAST OREGONIAN—
MAY 22, 1985

Lack of Business Closes Livestock Yard

The Baker Livestock Exchange, which in 1983 was the leading sales yard in Oregon, has closed. Owner Bob Hodnefield of La Grande said he was losing money on the business, making it impossible to keep it operating.

These migrant workers are harvesting onions on the McGill Farm near Marion in Marion County, Oregon. Bins filled with onions are spaced all over the field waiting to be picked up. This photo was taken on September 30, 1962—courtesy Salem Public Library

Packing filberts after they've been graded in 1937. The man in the middle isn't stealing a snack, he is a state inspector, checking the quality of the hazelnuts—courtesy Oregon State Library

the hazelnuts produced in the United States. There are nearly four million hazelnut trees in Oregon. It's an industry that provides jobs for people like the Hilles. John Rickard—the man who commuted to work by walking thirty-eight miles each way in 1853 (page 29)—has descendants who returned to the homestead many years later to work the land in a new way.

Sally and Rob Hilles—Growing Hazelnuts

Sally Hilles talks as she peers over the side of a huge vat of chocolate: "I feel like a modern pioneer. When we came up here, we started with a camper. The road was a bunny trail coming in. There were no buildings, no electricity, no underground irrigation. So we built roads, built buildings, started all of our trees from little tiny cuttings." She's remembering the turn of the millennium when she and her husband, Rob, returned to the family's 225 acres in Benton County near Corvallis.

Like her great-great-grandfather, John Rickard, Sally commuted from the property to a second job as she and Rob got started on their dream of raising hazelnuts on the family farm. For eleven years, she worked in the human resources section of Sacred Heart Hospital in Eugene. The couple planted trees—and waited.

In 1986, the hazelnut industry in Oregon suffered a blight that destroyed many orchards. The Hilleses therefore worked on raising a blight-resistant tree. They created a nursery that produces thirty thousand trees a year, to be planted on their own farm or sold to other growers.

Over time, the business has expanded dramatically. Sally and Rob moved from simply growing hazelnuts and trees to roasting the nuts and making candy. That's why Sally now stands over that vat of chocolate. She runs the shop, blends the chocolate and candies, and packages them up for sale. A few years ago, the couple decided to try a new marketing technique, selling their products over the Internet. It was so successful that they couldn't keep up with the demand for their Hazelnut Hill products. From January through September, the staff is small, consisting of Sally, Rob, and one full-time employee. But when October hits, so do the orders.

Sally cooks only when orders come in, because she doesn't use preservatives. She starts early in the morning, cooking fifty-pound batches of toffees and brittles along with the chocolate. The more orders come in, the earlier she starts and the later she works. For weeks at a time, she'll sleep only five hours a night just to keep up during the busy season. "I tease people that the only time I get a vacation is when the tractor breaks down and I have to go to the tractor store." As Sally's sleep decreases, the staff increases. Five clerks, ten packagers, and three shippers join the crew.

Even with all the hard work, Sally says it isn't about the hazelnuts as much as the people she sells them to. "I always tell people it's not about the nuts and candies," she says. "It's definitely about the relationships that we have with our customers and our different vendors that we work with."

It's also about the land. Sally is very mindful of the stewardship responsibilities she has, caring for the same acreage her ancestors settled when Oregon was not yet a state. John Rickard had no idea what effects his farming had on the land or the environment, but the Hilleses do, and they take that responsibility very seriously. Sally simply says, "We love every time we plant a tree how much carbon is being sequestered—the footprint that that provides, we feel like we're doing something good for the earth."

Though he is long gone, some of John Rickard's legacy lives on, not just in the land he farmed over a hundred and fifty years ago, but also in his great-great-granddaughter:

Sally Hilles prepares chocolate to coat the hazelnuts she grows—photo taken by Tom Fuller

Hazelnut orchard near Monroe, Oregon—photo taken by Tom Fuller

Rob and I both have the pioneer spirit. I would define it as not being set in conditioned thinking—being able to expand beyond what you think your own boundaries are and become comfortable with uncomfortable. You're not always going to have the means, the resources. You're not going to be the one out there on the golf course. You're not going to be the one doing what normal people do. But because of that you stretch yourself beyond what you think you can do. I know that this process has transformed me. I'm not the same person I was a few years back, even yesterday. Every day there's a challenge, and every day it transforms me, and every day I look forward to it.

Brewing and Winemaking in Oregon

Brewing

Since the late 1800s, the Willamette Valley has been a major national center for growing hops; the flower cone of the hops plant gives beer its distinctive flavor, aroma, and bitterness. With a plentiful local supply of hops and grains, Oregonians have been brewing beer since the state's early days. Henry Weinhard was one of Oregon's most notable early brewers. He established a brewery in Portland in the 1860s and by 1875 was shipping beer across the United States and even to Asia.

From 1920 to 1933, Prohibition banned the manufacture, transportation, and sale of alcohol for consumption. Historians say such activities continued, mostly hidden from public view. After the repeal of Prohibition, Oregon's legal production of beer resumed. However, it wasn't until the 1980s that Oregon's brewery industry began its rise from relative obscurity to world renown.

In the early 1980s, a group of pioneering microbrewers noticed Oregon shared some characteristics with Germany, including latitude, climate, and access to premium hops. In 1984 Rob Widmer, along with his brother and father, opened Widmer Brothers Brewing Co. in Portland. In 1985, the company produced four hundred barrels of beer.

That same year, the Oregon legislative assembly repealed Prohibition-era legislation that had banned the concept of a brewpub. This allowed Mike and Brian McMenamin to open Oregon's first brewpub, the Hillsdale Pub. Since then, Oregon has become

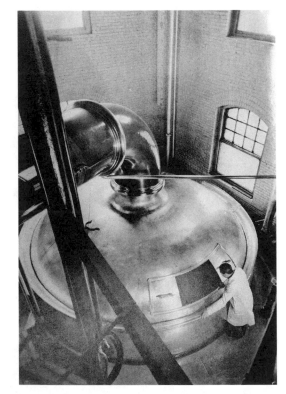

Man looks inside what is called "the West's largest brewing kettle" during the 1930s in Portland—courtesy Oregon State Library

Capital Brewery in Salem, ca 1880s—courtesy Oregon State Library

regarded as a center for the brewing and brewpub industry. In 2008, Oregon had sixty-one brewing companies operating ninety-two brewing facilities. The Portland area had the most breweries of any metro area in the world.

The brewing process requires patience and attention to detail. It takes time to learn the craft, whether by brewing beer at home in small batches or by working at a commercial brewery. There's a wide range of things to do in a brewery, and everything from cleaning kegs and equipment to working in the warehouse to bartending is common. But the heart of any beer brewing operation is the brewer.

Brewers select, prepare, and combine hops, malted grains, and yeast in varying quantities to create unique and marketable beer. They ensure quality by sterilizing equipment and by monitoring and controlling the whole brewing process, from crushing the malt and mixing it with warm water to fermenting and bottling the beer. They also analyze test samples. Brewers of fine beers must understand many technical details, such as temperatures for primary fermentation, priming sugars, alcohol

The 1971 Honeywood Winery booth at the Oregon State Fair. Bottles and glasses containing samples of the winery's fruit and berry wines are displayed on a board resting on three wine kegs—courtesy Oregon State Fair

This photo shows a driver (unknown) pulling picking bins full of Pinot Noir through the organic certified Pinot Noir block at the Estate Vineyard in Turner. Pickers unload their buckets of fruit into these picking bins, which are then delivered to the crush pad of the winery—courtesy Willamette Valley Vineyard

content, and the weight of hops. While the basics of making beer is simple—yeast digests sugars and produces alcohol—creating beer with exceptional flavor is an art.

Winemaking

As with beer, Oregonians have been making wine since the early territorial days. However, this activity diminished in the early 1900s because of competition from California's wine industry, the growth of the Temperance Movement, and Prohibition.

In the 1960s, Oregon's wine industry began growing again. A decade later, it adopted strict labeling standards, and since then, growth has been very rapid. The state had five wineries in 1970, one hundred in 1998, and three hundred fifty in 2006. Oregon's winemakers supervised the production of over a million and a half cases of wine in 2006, worth nearly $200 million. The state has become known worldwide for its fine Pinot Noir, but also produces wine from more than seventy other grape varieties, such as Pinot Gris, Chardonnay, and Riesling.

There are many jobs in a winery, and it's common for a winemaker to have done them all, according to Paul Gallick, of Honeywood Winery in Salem. Honeywood's winemaker apprenticed for years under the head winemaker and took correspondence courses at the University of California Davis during that time.

Winemakers participate in all stages of wine production. If the winery has a vineyard, this includes deciding the timing of the harvest and hiring helpers to pick the grapes. If the winery lacks a vineyard, the winemaker selects and buys the fruit. Then he or she supervises and participates in all the jobs in the winery. Family members often help with winemaking.

Winemakers sort, crush, and press the fruit. Long days and heavy lifting are common during the peak of the harvest season. As in the making of beer, sterilization of equipment is essential. Winemakers monitor and control the fermenting process and bottle the resulting wine. Those wishing to make fine wines learn to keep detailed records of the process and may seek the advice of a professional enologist (a specialist in winemaking) to get the taste just right. Marketing is another important task. This typically includes selecting bottles, designing a label, traveling to wine-tasting events, and opening and operating a tasting room. When other duties are done, the winemaker repairs barrels, fixes pumps, and prepares for next year's crop.

Manufacturing

In 1959, as Oregon celebrated its one hundredth birthday, almost three in ten off-the-farm jobs were in manufacturing. By 2007, that share had fallen to about one in ten. The biggest reason for the decline was the rapid increase of non-manufacturing jobs, which more than quadrupled from 351,500 in 1959 to 1,527,300 in 2007. Another reason for manufacturing's falling share was a large decline in the number of logging and wood-product manufacturing jobs; these fell in number by more than half, from 75,000 in 1959 to fewer than 37,000 in 2007.

Overall, the number of manufacturing jobs grew from 138,000 in 1950 to just over 204,000 in 2007. Oregon's high-tech firms were a major reason for this growth. High technology provided 1,400 jobs in 1955, compared to over 40,000 jobs in 2007.

Some of Oregon's more famous high-tech manufacturers—such as Intel—came here relatively recently. Others have been here a very long time. One such company began in downtown Portland when Oregon was only six years old.

Sulzer Pumps Mechanic—Bill Anderson
The blue monster dwarfs Bill Anderson. Perched over the immense curves and tubes of steel, Bill tries to contain the monster with a giant pneumatic wrench, turning huge bolts in just the right order. In a few days, this several-ton behemoth of a pump will be rushed off to a company or public works project somewhere to shuttle water or some other liquid from one place to another.

Bill Anderson is a mechanic at Sulzer Pumps on Portland's waterfront. Today, Sulzer is part of a fairly small segment of the equipment-manufacturing companies in Oregon. Only around five hundred people work in the industry statewide. But Sulzer's history stretches way back in Oregon history, and the number of men and women who have worked here has varied widely.

The company went into business in 1865 as Willamette Iron Works. Initially, Willamette Iron Works manufactured practically anything made from iron or steel. Around the turn of the century, they relocated to the banks of the Willamette and specialized in ship repair and creating steam-powered donkeys used in the logging industry (see a picture of one of their machines on page 94). By 1930, they'd built over three thousand of these powerful steam engines.

Machine worker in the 1980s—courtesy Oregon Employment Department

An employee of Gunderson Incorporated in Portland welds parts of a railroad car—courtesy Oregon Employment Department

Bill Anderson comes from a long line of employees at Sulzer Pumps. Here he inspects one of the giant pumps the company makes—photo taken by Tom Fuller

Employees of Willamette Irons Works (the predecessor of Sulzer Pumps) pose outside of their Portland business in 1877—courtesy Sulzer Pumps

The Great Depression virtually shut down the timber industry in Oregon, and with it, the need for Willamette's steam engines. World War II changed everything for the company, which had changed its name to Willamette Iron and Steel Corporation. Building warships swelled the company's employees from a handful of shipbuilders to thirty-six thousand at the height of the war effort. By the war's end in 1945, Willamette had built or converted seventy-eight naval vessels. (Read about Augusta Clawson, one of the people who built ships in Portland during World War II, on page 110.)

The '50s and '60s saw the company shift its emphasis to building pumps for the burgeoning nuclear power industry. That's when John Frazee, Bill's grandfather, started working. Then in the early '70s Bill's dad, Bill Anderson Sr., started at the company as a test mechanic.

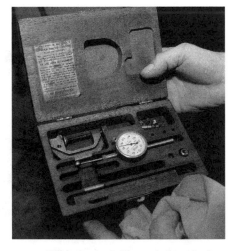

Bill Anderson holds a set of test tools his grandfather left him—photo taken by Tom Fuller

Bill Jr. still has his grandfather's test kit. The dial indicator on the large tool in the center was used to check whether a part was properly centered and installed. Bill's grandfather made $3.00 an hour. Today's mechanics usually make around $18.00 for that same hour of work.

The tools are different today as well. Hydraulics were used to power the wrenches, or they would use something called a slug wrench, a large wrench with a knob on the end that they would hit with a hammer. Now compressed air drives all the tools, which is known as pneumatics.

It takes about six days for Sulzer to put together one of these giant pumps. It used to be the company competed on price and capacity. In today's global market, Sulzer competes on efficiency—how fast they can put pumps together and get them to the customer. Sulzer now ships pumps all over the world and despite its small size, leads the industry.

Another person who worked for Sulzer, back when it was Willamette Iron and Steel, was Shirley Burnett. That is to say, he worked for Willamette when he wasn't fighting milk cows on his farm.

Mechanical Engineer & Farmer—Shirley Burnett

The smell of fresh-cut hay followed Shirley Burnett into the house. After a long day running his baler around neighbors' farms, Shirley arrived back at the family farm in Eagle Creek only to realize he had to turn around and milk the cows—a twice-daily chore that was getting on his nerves. "That's it," he said firmly to anyone who would listen. "I'm going to sell those cows and from now on we can just buy milk at the grocery store."

Since 1945, Shirley Burnett had farmed one hundred acres of the original 640-acre farm of Philip Foster (his great-grandfather, whose story is on page 58). Those one hundred acres had been purchased back by Shirley's dad, Gus Burnett (whose story can be found on page 92). In addition, he leased and worked another hundred acres nearby. Shirley was particularly proud of his five acres of loganberries, a cross between a raspberry and a blackberry. He had done all the work of digging the postholes, splitting nine hundred posts, and running twenty miles of wire to hold the berries. It had been hard work, but the soft soil of the Philip Foster Farm made it possible.

He also raised sheep and, during lambing season, he would go out to the barn, even in the middle of the night in freezing weather, to assist the ewes giving birth. But farming just didn't bring in that much money. So Shirley supplemented his income by custom-baling hay and combining grains. He would bring in 12.5 cents a bale, good money for baling hay in those days (this was about $1.50 in 2008 dollars). The problem was that he often ended up working for others until 9:30 at night during the season and having to come home to milk the cows cut into that time. The cows had to go.

By 1959, Shirley had almost given up farming anyway. His daughter Joanne (whose story is on page 165) was in college. In order to pay for that education, Shirley returned to a career he started many years before—engineering.

Shirley Burnett as a young man—courtesy Joanne Broadhurst and Tom Burnett

Shirley Burnett and his grandson ride on a tractor on the Burnett farm, ca late 1960s—courtesy of Joanne Broadhurst and Tom Burnett

Shirley Burnett worked as a materials engineer for what was to become Sulzer Pumps—courtesy of Joanne Broadhurst and Tom Burnett

Margaret Pritchard worked as an engineer for Portland General Electric in the 1950s—courtesy Margaret Pritchard

While at Willamette Iron and Steel, Shirley made good use of his degree from Oregon State College. In addition to pumps, the company made such things as dam gates for the Grand Coulee Dam and valves for the New York City sewer system.

Shirley was a materials engineer. After the company acquired a bid, Shirley determined exactly what materials they needed and where to purchase them. At one point, Shirley inherited a big problem. Someone had grossly underbid on a project. Shirley's task was to make sure they completed the job without losing the company money. So he found materials at a better price and figured out a more efficient process to manufacture the parts, and they came in at the bid price.

Engineer—Margaret Pritchard

When did Margaret Pritchard become an engineer? To hear her tell it, it was at age three. It was about that time that her mother caught young Margaret taking her brother's clock apart. "I was just opening up the main spring when Mother caught me," she remembers. "She made me put it back in working order by dinner time, and I did."

Margaret's mother was none other than Laverne Pritchard, one of Oregon's first female bank managers (read her story on page 85), and her grandmother was Edna Hershner, the woman who saved up her egg and butter money to start investing in real estate. (Read her story on page 86.) So it's not surprising that Margaret would want to break ground in what was a traditionally male field.

Margaret's predilection towards engineering never wavered. When she was six years old, she asked her parents to return a doll set given to her and exchange it for a carpenter set. When she was in high school in Milwaukie, she asked to take math rather than home or commercial economics. Laverne appealed to the school board and Margaret got her classes in mechanical drawing and higher math.

Margaret was offered a full scholarship to college but couldn't take it because she was needed at home to help care for her family. She went to night school instead at Multnomah Junior College to study engineering, and in 1958 she began working during the day at Portland General Electric. Despite her talent and training, Margaret remembers being paid $2,500.00 a year less than her male counterparts.

The inequality of pay between men and women has existed in America throughout its history, but it wasn't until 1964 that something was done about it. That year, President John F. Kennedy signed the Equal Pay Act into law. This law made it illegal to pay women and men differently for the same job solely because of gender. Up until that time newspapers printed separate job listings for men and women. Between 1960 and 1964, women with full-time year-round jobs earned, on average, $0.60 for every $1.00 earned by men in full-time year-round jobs

Pay wasn't the only disparity for Margaret Pritchard. Her duties included mapping and tax calculations. Male linesmen would string power lines along a road. They would generate a report and bring it back to Margaret's office. She would draw a line on a map to indicate the type and distance of the new line.

> I would get a hold of that map and calculate the wire miles. I would put a wheel along the map that would read the miles. If there was something that didn't fit right, I'd call back to the service center to see which was which. I was the court of last resort, but I was not allowed out on the line myself. I stayed in the office with the other women workers.

Margaret remembers working in that service center for thirty-six hours straight answering the telephone during the Columbus Day storm in 1962. But even if she had wanted to, Margaret could not leave the office to help customers with downed lines. That was a man's job.

Margaret Pritchard (third woman from the front) works in the offices of PGE in the 1950s—courtesy Margaret Pritchard

Working in an Aluminum Factory

The construction of Bonneville Dam during the Great Depression led to cheap hydroelectric power for businesses. The availability of this inexpensive power led to the creation of several aluminum mills situated along the Columbia River. The creation of the mills, in turn, led to increased employment. By the early 1950s, there were many workers tending the molten ore.

A major job in the aluminum factories was that of pot-tender. A pot-tender monitored the progress of the smelting done in "pots," which were large troughs lined with metal. After a tapping crew removed the molten aluminum from the pot's prior smelting, a new charge of ore was delivered to the pot by an overhead conveyor belt or a special ore truck.

In one common process, the pot-tender then lowered large carbon blocks, about one foot square each, into the ore. These blocks—known as carbons—were electrodes attached to a source of very powerful electricity. As the electricity flowed through the carbon and into the ore, it heated the ore to more than 1,800 degrees

Fahrenheit and reduced it to a molten state from which aluminum could be strained. In another process, a slurry of carbon briquettes served as the electrical contact that helped smelt the ore.

In both processes, it was a hot job working near the slowly melting ore, hurrying from one end to the other to break up the crust forming on the surface and to be sure the carbon electrodes were positioned at the correct depth and drawing the correct amount of current. If a carbon needed adjustment, pot-tenders turned a control wheel to raise or lower the carbon, or used a long rod to move it slightly so it would make better contact with the surrounding ore. Sometimes a pot-tender would tend two pots at once, rushing back and forth between them to make sure the refining process was proceeding as desired. For protection, workers wore leather gloves with long gauntlets and leather bib-overalls.

The mill operated three eight-hour shifts per day. Because each charge in a pot took substantially longer than one eight-hour shift to fully melt, a pot-tender would not necessarily see his pot emptied and re-charged every day.

Aluminum smelter jobs no longer exist in Oregon. The last operating smelters began closing around 2000 as electricity prices spiked (due to the California electricity crisis), foreign competition grew stiffer, and company officials decided that the aging plants were no longer competitive.

Truck Driving

For many years after the automobile first plied the roads of Oregon, the work of hauling goods was still done by horse and wagon. It wasn't until after World War I that trucks became more common and accepted. Prior to the war, only about one hundred thousand trucks were produced a year in America. After the war, that number jumped to over half a million. So now there were numerous trucks on the roads, but there weren't numerous roads for the trucks.

Without a good road system, most freight still moved by rail. This was the state of things all the way up until the creation of the interstate highway system in the 1940s and '50s. The ribbons of concrete and asphalt connecting major U.S. cities made transporting goods by long-haul truck very affordable. All of those trucks needed drivers. By 1950, truck and tractor drivers were among the top ten occupations in Oregon.

Those 1950s-era long-haul trucks were notoriously difficult to operate and had few amenities. Better technology has improved handling, efficiency, and safety, but driving a big rig is still a risky occupation. Truck drivers can spend up to eleven hours per day behind the wheel and up to fourteen hours engaged in some sort of activity involving their truck or cargo. These duties include fueling, filling out paperwork, overseeing repairs, and undergoing mandatory inspections. A trucker can expect to spend weeks away from home. Operating an eighty-thousand-pound, sixty-foot-long eighteen-wheeler can be dangerous.

A truck with a load of hop sacks. A man by the name of J.D. King is sitting on top of the stack, ca 1920–1930—courtesy Oregon State Library

Truck drivers account for 12 percent of all work-related deaths, which is more than any other profession. They are five times more likely to die on the job than the average worker.

State and federal laws limit the number of hours a trucker can spend driving and be on duty in any twenty-four-hour period. They must record in a logbook their hours driving, their payload, origin and destination, and daily mileage.

Around 1950, the twenty thousand or so truckers in Oregon earned about $3,100.00 a year (that's the equivalent of $27,000.00 today). By the twenty-first century, the number of jobs for truckers had increased to more than twenty-five thousand. Average pay for the driver of a heavy tractor-trailer today is about $37,000.00 a year.

Truck inspector tests the load on an axle at an Oregon weigh station, ca late 1940s—courtesy Oregon State Archives

Waste Management

Every day the average Oregonian creates four-and-a-half pounds of waste—that's five million tons a year from the state. As landfills are filled and concerns about leaks from those landfills increase, many Oregon communities have begun recycling programs in earnest. As of 2006, just over half of the waste generated in the Portland metropolitan area was recovered or prevented by recycling programs.

Recycling and waste management employs over sixteen hundred people in Oregon. One of them is Austin Warner. The name may be familiar. Austin's dad, Austin Carl Warner, lives on the farm of Carlton founder Wilson Carl (see Austin Carl Warner's story on page 129, and Wilson Carl's story on page 21). Austin worked the farm as a boy.

Long haul trucker for May Trucking Company pulls out of a depot at Brooks, Oregon—photo taken by Tom Fuller

Austin Warner picks up a garbage can along his route in McMinnville—photo taken by Tom Fuller

Austin Warner

The farm just didn't produce enough income to support him, so young Austin went to work at a local meat packing plant. When an on-the-job injury kept him from continuing in that line of work, he took a position at Oregon Waste Management in McMinnville.

You could call Austin a garbage hauler, but these days a lot of what Austin picks up is not going into a landfill. Instead it is recyclable material that will be sorted and sent to various companies who can turn it back into useable products.

Austin's day starts pretty early as he drives around McMinnville. In the mid-twentieth century, it wasn't uncommon to see workers picking up metal garbage cans by hand and emptying their contents into the back of a compactor. These days, the truck does all the heavy lifting. Austin positions his vehicle close to the curb and sends out a special device to pick up the trash and recycling and dump it in the back. Special cameras let Austin track everything happening outside while he stays in the cab. In the coming decade, employment in this industry will grow by about 20 percent, a little faster than the economy as a whole, because of limitations on landfills and the requirements of higher levels of recycling.

Austin still does a few things around the farm, but most of the land has been rented out to others. These days he's fixing up the old farmhouse where generations of the Carl family got their start.

The Service Sector

Over the last fifty years, the total employment share of most non-manufacturing industries in Oregon grew. The reason? Automation of agriculture and manufacturing allowed—and required—workers to seek employment in other industries. Automation of some household chores also encouraged women to enter the labor force. In the 1950s, the service sector accounted for only about 12 percent of employment, but a group of roughly comparable industries in 2007 accounted for about 39 percent of all jobs. Employment in industries such as finance (like working at a bank, for example, or as a tax preparer), insurance, and realty employment grew from 4 percent to 6 percent. Construction jobs rose from 5 percent to 6 percent. However, two non-manufacturing sectors became less prominent during the past half-century: federal government jobs dropped from 4 percent to 2 percent, and retail trade fell from 16 percent to 12 percent.

Unidentified woman goes through a training course to be a waitress in 1963—courtesy Oregon Employment Department

An Oregon Retail Tradition—Meier & Frank

October 27, 2007, was a big day in Portland. That morning, about two hundred people lined up for the re-opening of a city landmark. The downtown building known for generations as Meier & Frank would open its doors under another historic name: Macy's. The history of Meier & Frank begins before Oregon was officially a state.

Meier & Frank dates back to 1857 when Aaron Meier opened a thirty-five- by fifty-foot mercantile on Front Street. At that time, Portland's population was only thirteen hundred people. After Meier partnered with Emil Frank in 1870, the store became known as Meier & Frank.

Meier & Frank quickly became a Portland tradition. At one time, it had the tallest building in the Pacific Northwest. During the Great Depression, the store took out a full page ad reading simply, "Confidence." Hundreds brought their savings to the store for safe keeping, and the store even canceled interest charges on store accounts for a time. During World War II, federal officials cited the store for its major contributions to the war efforts.

In the mid-twentieth century, Meier & Frank was a destination not only as a place to buy clothes and shoes, but also as a place to get a good meal.

Meier & Frank store in Salem in 1959—courtesy Oregon State Library

Meier & Frank sale, ca 1950s. Notice the sign on the counter, offering Crepe Blouses for $2.99—courtesy Macy's

	Top Occupations in 2006		
1	Sales representatives and retail sales workers	141,199	8%
2	Office clerks, secretaries, and administrative assistants	85,384	5%
3	Combined food preparation and service workers, including fast food	33,639	2%
4	Bookkeeping, accounting, and auditing clerks	28,268	2%
5	Registered nurses	27,988	2%
6	Agricultural workers	27,573	2%
7	Waiters and waitresses	27,367	2%
8	Hand laborers and freight, stock, and material movers	26,202	1%
9	Truck drivers, heavy and tractor-trailer	25,480	1%
10	Customer service representatives	23,420	1%
11	Janitors and cleaners	23,120	1%
12	General and operations managers	20,549	1%

Chef—Howard Woodward

Three in the morning always came early for Howard Woodward. After dragging himself out of bed, Howard had to get himself out the door and onto a Portland city bus. He would ride to SW Fifth and Alder to arrive at 4 AM sharp at the kitchen door of Meier & Frank. In the custom of the day, Howard arrived in hat, white shirt, tie, and overcoat. It was only after entering the kitchen that Howard would put on his chef's apron and hat.

From the early 1900s through the 1950s, department-store tea rooms enjoyed a huge popularity. The Tea Room at Meier & Frank was even mentioned as one of the top dining spots in the city, if not the entire Pacific Coast.

In his position as chef, Howard had to heat up the huge ovens in the tenth floor tearoom kitchen and see that the meats and produce were brought out for the day's menu. He helped direct a large staff who made salads, pies, and cakes. Howard also created meals for company picnics and Christmas parties. Howard's W-2 from 1959 shows he earned $3,241.00 that year.

Adjacent to the Tea Room was the Georgian Room (a private dining room) and the Pine Room, which Portlanders knew as the Men's Grill. It was a popular place for Portland businessmen to meet. The Tea Room was known for its delicious food, prepared by chefs like Howard Woodward under the watchful eye of the Frank family. At some point, all the rooms became known as the Georgian Room.

Howard Woodward serves at a Meier & Frank picnic in 1952—courtesy Shirley Schwartz

Another business with a long history in Oregon is U.S. Bank, which started life as United States National Bank of Portland, in 1891. Over the years, U.S. Bank has provided jobs for many tellers and managers, as well as loans for many Oregon businesses and individuals. One of those who oversaw that process is himself part of Oregon history.

Bank Manager—Curtis Tigard

When we last saw Curtis Tigard, he was selling newspapers for $0.03 a piece on the corner of a downtown Portland Farmer's Market in the early 1900s (that story is on page 99). Fast-forward to the 1950s, and Curtis is managing the U.S. National Bank Tigard branch. The city of Tigard gets its name from Curtis's grandfather, Wilson Tigard, who settled in the area in the 1850s. (See Wilson's and his son Charles's stories on page 98.)

Curtis Tigard in the 1950s—courtesy David Tigard

Curtis earned $10,000.00 to $12,000.00 a year as bank manager, which was good money in the 1950s. He worked regular hours, from eight to five. Curtis's main job was to supervise his employees and decide whether the bank would give out loans.

Typically, customers asked for up to $500.00 for a personal loan, and up to $10,000.00 for a mortgage loan. The interest rate was somewhere between 8 and 10 percent for personal loans and 6 percent for real estate. The most difficult part of Curtis's job was collecting on those loans when people didn't pay. He'd head out of the office and go to their homes or places of business to ask them about it personally.

Store Owners—Ann Horton

In the late 1950s, Ann Horton faced a dilemma. As a single mom with two children, she had twice as much work to do to keep her family thriving. As the co-owner of a small business in Medford, Oregon, she had the responsibility of keeping her store profitable.

Ann's grandfather opened Lawrence's Jewelers after arriving in Oregon by train in 1908 (John Lawrence's story is on page 97). Ann had worked in the family business since she was thirteen years old. She started out by cleaning up and doing some selling. By 1959, she was almost thirty, and now co-owned the place with her mother, father, and brother.

Ann's son Jerry was just a toddler at this time, so Ann brought in a babysitter to watch the kids while she worked at the store. It was a small place as Ann remembers, more of a closet than a store. While her brother Bob repaired watches, Ann looked through catalogs trying

Ann Horton and son Chuck pose for a picture in the store in 1964—courtesy Ann Horton

Lawrence's Jewelers in the 1950s—courtesy Ann Horton

to figure out what would catch her customers' fancies. "I wanted our store to be the Tiffany of Medford," Ann says of that time. "I would have vendors come in with samples, especially china and silver. I'd pick what would sell and what our budget could afford."

Ann built up her clientele mainly through weddings, though she came up with other methods to attract customers as well. One of the promotions Ann came up with was to give a silver teaspoon to each girl graduating from high school. In the 1950s the spoons she gave out cost about $1.25 (today for a good silver teaspoon you might pay anywhere from $6.95 to over $70.00). As prices rose, this promotion became more and more difficult. "We ended up having to give out smaller and smaller spoons as they became more expensive."

Ann learned to juggle her dual roles of mom and business owner, in part, by combining them. Each year, a trade show in San Francisco provided a great opportunity to see both the latest in jewelry and a major league baseball game. So Ann took her sons down to California, and while they went to the ballpark, she went to the show.

In the 1950s, downtowns were still the core shopping areas for most towns and cities. Large shopping malls had not yet cropped up. When that happened in the 1970s and '80s, it changed many things, but not the way Ann ran her business:

> My grandfather always had the best advice—"don't worry about your competitors, worry about yourself. Take care of your business. This goes well despite what changes in the world. Make sure it's doing the right things for your customer. Honesty is the best policy. The customer is always right even though they might be wrong."

Ann passed on this advice to her son, Jerry, who started working in the store in 1970 at the age of fourteen. Today, he runs the business and has taken over the repair work for his uncle Bob.

Jerry Higginbotham

Jerry didn't start out wanting to go into the family business. He wanted to be a musician, but when that didn't work out, he came back to the store full time. "It was something I could do, and it was easy for me to just stay here and do that. It means more to me now than it did then."

Jerry is now happy with his choice and finds himself becoming less shy and more comfortable around the customers. He sits behind the counter at his tool bench, using some of the same files and tools his great-grandfather used when he opened the store in 1908. He

Inside Lawrence's Jewelers in the late 1940s and 1950s. Some of the same display cases are still used in the store today—courtesy Ann Horton

enjoys taking things apart, fixing what's broken, and then trying to put it back together again. If he can't fix, it he sends the piece to someone who can.

A sense of history and continuity pervades Lawrence's Jewelers. Some of the display cabinets are clearly antiques, and the family has a way of doing business that seems oddly out of place in today's world, yet fits right in with the tradition of service to the customer first.

Like his mother, Ann, Jerry also believes in Great-Grandpa John Lawrence's advice, saying, "Our slogan is 'doing things the old-fashioned way,' taking somebody at his word. Your handshake is as good as we need. We try to treat everyone that way."

In a world where many people no longer venture downtown to shop, Jerry and Ann must work harder to keep the store open into its second century. Part of their secret is finding a niche that mall stores cannot fill. Then they "wow" their customers with extras like free gift-wrapping, free shipping with a minimum order, and free repairs if the job is small enough. "I love it when someone comes in for a minor repair and I can fix it quickly and not charge them. 'You don't want to charge me?' they say. 'No, it's too easy.'"

Ann Horton still works at the store, inspecting diamonds and keeping the books—photo taken by Tom Fuller

The High-Tech Industry

Computer and electronic equipment manufacturing has been a prominent activity in Oregon since the 1970s. Tektronix was founded in Oregon in 1946. Both Intel and Hewlett-Packard arrived in 1976. By the early 1980s, Tektronix employed as many as twenty-four thousand workers, though employment thereafter declined due to spin-offs and strong competition. Intel grew in the 1990s to take Tektronix's place as the state's largest industrial employer. By the late 1990s, high-tech employment of seventy thousand had surpassed forest products jobs in Oregon.

Tektronix

When Howard Vollum envisioned a new oscilloscope in the mid-1940s, he had no idea that he was giving birth to Oregon's high-tech industry. During World War II, Howard worked with radar. The measurement instruments used were crude and limited. Though he didn't foresee the phenomena of television and computers, both of these required an instrument that could measure events happening very fast or at irregular intervals.

OREGONIAN—OCTOBER 8, 1985

Motorola plans to close Beaverton software lab

Company changes at the regional and national levels forced Motorola/Four-Phase Systems Inc. to close a computer programs manufacturing plant in Beaverton. Decreases in demand had already caused the company to lay off half of the employees at the location.

Howard Vollum, co-founder of Tektronix—courtesy Tektronix

So Howard purchased surplus war parts for a fraction of their value and began assembling a better measurement instrument on a piece of plywood he called a breadboard. When he finished with the 501 (affectionately called the Vollumscope) it took up his entire workbench. The 501 was a breakthrough technologically but was far too large and clumsy to market. After redesigning the 501's appearance, the new company released its first product, the 511.

A peek inside the shop and assembly line at the early Tektronix plant reveals a place very different from high-tech factories of today. Workers wore casual clothes. They stood or sat at large tables assembling products by hand. High-tech manufacturing has come a long way since then.

High-Tech Jobs in the Twenty-First Century

In Oregon's large semiconductor manufacturing industry, the most common occupations are semiconductor processors, engineers, and engineering technicians. These employees typically do much of their work in small teams of workers.

Semiconductor processors spend long hours in fabrication plants (fabs), standing in and slowly walking around ultra-clean rooms filled with highly complex equipment with which they make microprocessors and computer memory chips. While working in the clean rooms, they have to wear special clothing—often called bunny suits—along with hairnets, hoods, goggles, boots,

An Intel technician dons a "bunny suit" and uses a scanner to begin production of silicon wafers used to produce Intel computer chips—courtesy Intel

and if necessary even beard-covers to ensure that all of their clothing and hair is covered. This is to prevent dust from contaminating the chips, which would ruin them. The lightweight suits are fairly comfortable, and the factory air temperature is carefully controlled.

These factories operate around the clock and people typically work in shifts—in some cases, twelve-hour shifts with rotating day and night schedules and lengthy periods of days off. Intel says it offers a variety of work schedules to address both business and employee needs, such as compressed workweeks, alternative start times, part-time positions, and telecommuting.

Technology in the Workplace

Very few things have changed how people work like the advent of the personal computer. In the 1950s and '60s, most organizations had steno pools—groups of employed secretaries that knew stenography. There were even classes at business colleges that taught how to write in shorthand, a series of lines, curves, and other marks that allowed someone to take down a letter or memo as it was dictated, then later transcribe it onto paper using a manual typewriter.

Those who didn't have stenographers would write out their letters and correspondences in longhand and then hand that paper to a secretary, or send it to the typing pool, where someone would type up the letter, return it to the requester for changes, and then retype it for mailing or filing—a process that could take days or weeks. Electric typewriters made the task somewhat easier, but the focus on paper and carbon copies meant a lot of jobs for people creating, editing, mailing, and filing paper.

Beginning in the late '70s and early '80s, the personal computer changed all of that. Though several manufacturers released small microcomputers around the same time, the IBM Personal Computer gained a foothold in the business world. These first computers were very slow by today's standards, but the ability to create, edit, and print documents from a desk revolutionized the office.

Each year, computers got faster, with more memory and more office productivity software available. Computer networks linked individual computers together, allowing file sharing and greater storage.

Seven women typing in a stenographic pool as part of the Works Progress Administration Federal Writers' Project in March of 1937—courtesy Oregon State Library

Clerical workers at Marion County, Oregon, Health Demonstration Project, 1926—courtesy Oregon State Archives

Unidentified man sits at computer in the late 1970s—courtesy Oregon Employment Department

The 1990s saw the birth of intranets (networks within organizations) and the Internet, which allowed computers from all over the world to connect together.

Computers are now essential to the work most of us do. The number of people using personal computers at work more than doubled between 1984 and 2003, going from one in four to nearly six in ten. Computers have become so much a part of our work that every major occupation group has jobs that require computer skills. Nearly one quarter of all job openings in Oregon now require some kind of computer skills.

Today desktop and laptop computers have replaced many of the staple office items of most of the twentieth century. The word processor replaced the typewriter, e-mail has replaced postal mail and memos as the accepted communication tool for the office, computer spreadsheets have replaced adding machines, and online databases have relegated many filing cabinets to the basement storage room.

In some offices during the 1950s and '60s, managers recorded their voices onto wax cylinders, and later magnetic tape, which secretaries played back and typed onto paper. The Dictaphone was probably the most well-known device of this kind. As computers replaced typewriters, voice-recognition began to replace dictation and transcription. Today Dictaphone produces software and hardware to assist in the dictation of medical information for the health-care industry, as well as other applications.

Computers are getting smaller, as well. Devices such as the Blackberry® and the iPhone® have allowed some workers to take their work with them in their purses or on their belts. Mobile computing also allows more and more employees to work from home. High-speed Internet access, along with increased facility and transportation costs, have encouraged many businesses and even government agencies to create shorter workweeks and allow telecommuting.

Computers have brought their own set of problems into the workplace, though. While greatly increasing worker productivity, they also increase eye strain, muscle fatigue, and nerve damage. Sitting behind a computer screen all day also decreases the amount of physical activity a worker gets on the job. One study found that two-thirds of office employees reported physical ailments related to computer use. All those trips to the typing pool were actually good for us.

CORVALLIS GAZETTE-TIMES—
NOVEMBER 26, 1995

Labor Shortage Solutions: Firms Change Rules to Attract New Workers

Managers at Epson Portland Inc. were having a hard time finding enough qualified workers for their growing printer factory until they made a change in their conditions for employment. They stopped requiring that employees speak English. Since the change earlier this year, the company has been able to find all the employees it needs to double its work force to 2,000.

Baby Boomers

The many children born between 1946 and 1964—the baby boomers—began to enter the workforce in the 1960s. In addition to entering college in large numbers, they swelled the nation's pool of workers. The peak of the baby boom was in the 1950s; at this time, Oregon's employment was growing by an average of 1.8 percent per year. In the following decade—as the oldest boomers began entering the workforce and Oregon's plywood industry geared up to supply the demand for new homes, the state's job growth surged by an annual average of 3.6 percent.

In the 1970s, as the peak of the baby boom entered the workforce and the wood-products industry was operating at full throttle, Oregon's employment grew by an annual average of 4.1 percent. In the 1980s, the growth rate dipped to 1.4 percent as the influx of boomers into the workforce slowed to a trickle and a severe housing-related recession resulted in huge job losses in Oregon's construction and wood-products sectors. As the twentieth century drew to a close, and boomers were in their relatively stable mid-career years, Oregon's high-tech sector grew rapidly, pushing the job growth rate up to an average of 2.8 percent during the 1990s.

The oldest boomers turned sixty years old in 2006. This large demographic is already in, or is fast approaching, its late-career years. Will most boomers retire when they reach the age of sixty-five? Recent trends suggest that many of them will remain in the labor force past age sixty-five, either from economic necessity or for the pleasure of doing meaningful work.

The concept of meaningful work will only become more important. Some studies suggest that workers of the future will place just as much emphasis on how fulfilling work is as on how much they are paid. But work that is meaningful doesn't always pay well. In fact, sometimes, it doesn't pay at all. Just ask Christy Van Heukelem.

Librarian—Christy Van Heukelem

It's not an easy room to find. Down the stairs, around a number of corners, and through an archway is where the computer lab at the Salem Public Library can be found. The room consists of two rows of tables, each fitted with a computer and a flat screen monitor. About a dozen people sit at the PCs, but none touch the keyboards just yet. They're too busy listening to the story of how Christy Van Heukelem found her family.

This man participated in a training course for formal waiters in 1963—courtesy Oregon Employment Department

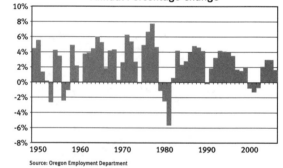

Oregon's Growth in Nonfarm Payroll Jobs Annual Percentage Change

Source: Oregon Employment Department

Christy Van Heukelem answers questions posed by members of a genealogy class taught in the basement of the Salem public library—photo taken by Tom Fuller

The William Hunt Wilson family reunion at Drain, Oregon in 1917—courtesy Christy Van Heukelem

Christy Van Heukelem shelves children's books at the Salem Public Library—photo taken by Tom Fuller

Just a few years ago, Christy tells the class, her family consisted of eleven people. "They could fit around a dining room table," she says. Then a box arrived from an uncle who had entered an Alzheimer's unit. Inside the box she found a very old picture of about seventy individuals sitting on a hillside.

Her mother identified some relatives by name, but the identities of most of the people in the picture were a mystery. All her mother knew was that the picture was taken in Drain, Oregon. Christy called the Douglas County Historical Society to inquire if anyone there could help her with her mysterious family picture. After she explained a few details, the person on the other end of the phone told her she had a treasure in her possession—a picture of the 1917 family reunion of Oregon pioneer William Hunt Wilson (see William's story on page 26).

That piece of information changed Christy's life. As the history unfolded, Christy's family grew from eleven to more than three thousand. She shares her story to encourage those in the computer lab to delve into their own genealogies. It's a perfect fit for a woman who trained and worked as a teacher, then started a long career in library service. What she didn't know was how closely her values matched those of the five generations of Oregonians who preceded her.

Later, Christy stares intently into the screen of her computer. She seems not to mind the king cobra sitting in her lap. Christy's just trying to find the right home for the snake. It isn't a *real* king cobra, of course, but a book about them. As a library associate for the Salem Public Library, Christy's day job is to purchase and catalog thousands of books like this each year. That way, library patrons can learn about cobras without venturing to southern Asia. When she's not teaching free classes on genealogy, she pours through shelf after shelf of books, making sure that when they go out into the main library, people can find them easily.

The library uses the Dewey Decimal System, which divides books by subject into numbered sections. Christy still uses the basic categories created by Melvil Dewey, who invented them in the time of Christy's Oregon pioneer ancestor William Hunt Wilson, though the categories have been expanded, so she can locate the exact numbers to use for the book on cobras.

Christy oversees purchasing operations for thousands of books each year. She and other staff members handle a portion of the process: ordering, receiving, cataloging, preparing, and shelving. Christy's responsibility also covers cataloging children's books. On a typical month during ordering season, she'll receive well over a thousand books, all of which she must categorize like the one on king cobras. Even when the library is closed, her work never stops. Christy describes one of her daily tasks:

> It's overwhelming. Too many things to do and not enough time to do it. Today I spent four hours searching paperbacks and putting them into our computer system. We have eighteen different libraries that use the same catalog, so I wanted to make sure we had one record for an item instead of eighteen.

Christy's been doing this job for twenty-four years. Before that, she worked as an elementary school teacher. In that nearly quarter-century, some things have stayed the same—like the Dewey Decimal System—but other things we consider commonplace are things that Dewey, or William Hunt Wilson, could never have imagined.

The Internet, for instance, now links all eighteen libraries so that customers can look up items in the catalog from their home and even reserve a book online. Christy believes that "Computers have helped us, because we are in the information age and libraries are all about information. We just have different tools today than we did. The computer is just a tool. You can use a tool for good or you can use it for bad." The Internet also links Christy to hundreds of her relatives across the country, and helps her further research the parents and siblings of William Hunt Wilson.

Learning about her ancestors has taught Christy more about herself than she imagined. Why did she go to college and become a teacher? William Hunt Wilson valued education highly, and helped found the first normal school in Drain, Oregon. His granddaughter, wife of Arthur Gardner (page 100), graduated from college, as did Arthur's daughter, wife of Chester Corry (page 105). Christy says the majority of the women in her family were teachers. She knew nothing of this until she dug into the family history.

A spiritual heritage also comes to her from William Hunt Wilson—through Arthur Gardner, a minister, to her grandparents, then her mother, and then to Christy. She graduated from Western Baptist College in Salem (now known as Corban College), and is very active in her church.

She looks back at the lives she has so recently discovered and feels a sense of continuity and pride in how belief can create a family destiny:

> To have ancestors that were ordinary people but did extraordinary things with their lives for the benefit of others is an honor. I realize that a lot of who I am is because of who they were. My value for education goes right back to William Hunt Wilson who said, 'They can steal the money you put in your pocket but they can't steal what you put in your head.'

That spirit continues in Christy today—that pioneer spirit first expressed by her great-great-great-grandfather, William Hunt Wilson, paraphrased by Christy:

> Work together to make life better. John McLoughlin—he gave of his own wealth to help these people who were almost destitute when they got here. During the depression people worked together to survive and sometimes that meant doing a job you didn't like, but you did it anyway because it needed to be done, and it provided income. I feel a responsibility of stewardship to the State of Oregon. Since my family has called this land "home" for so many years—I owe it to their memory to protect it and care for it.

The Lottery and Gambling

The state lottery was created in 1984 to strengthen Oregon's economy and create jobs. The lottery's creation also allowed Oregon's Native American tribes to operate casinos on tribal land. The first casino opened in 1994, and the number of casinos grew rapidly. By the end of 2004 there were nine casinos in Oregon. These businesses increased the presence of jobs such as gaming dealers (566 jobs in 2006), gaming cage workers (340 jobs), and gaming surveillance officers and investigators (302 jobs). With the success of tribal casinos and associated hotels and restaurants, Oregon's tribes have expanded to other enterprises such as running a truck stop, a specialty foods company, and a communications service. Employment at Native American tribal establishments grew from an average of thirty-two hundred jobs in 1995 to eighty-two hundred in 2007.

Labor Laws

During World War II, the U.S. government required defense contractors to treat workers of all races equally. However, this law didn't apply to other employers. It wasn't until 1964 that Congress passed sweeping legislation barring companies from discriminating in the employment of workers on the basis of race, gender, national origin, or religion.

In 1970, Congress gave workers over the age of forty legal protections against employment discrimination. Also in 1970, President Nixon signed the

Occupational Safety and Health Act (OSHA), creating standards for workplace safety and providing legal protection for whistle-blowers, workers who report workplace safety problems. In 1972, the 1964 anti-discrimination provisions were extended to employment by government agencies.

In 1981, another extension outlawed employment discrimination on the basis of pregnancy. The Immigration Reform and Control Act of 1986 prohibited some types of employment discrimination based on immigration status. The Americans with Disabilities Act of 1990 required employers to make reasonable accommodation on the job for workers with disabilities. The Civil Rights Act of 1991 added to employees' rights. Starting in 1993, the Family and Medical Leave Act (FMLA) required most employers to give eligible employees up to a total of twelve workweeks of unpaid leave per year to handle important family situations such as the birth and care of their newborn children, and to care for themselves or their immediate family members with serious health conditions.

Mike Zeazus works for the state of Oregon as a data processor in the early 1980s—courtesy Oregon Employment Department

Minimum wage laws also changed over the past half-century. In 1967, Oregon passed a minimum wage law that took effect February 1, 1968. The minimum hourly rates were $1.25 for adults and $1.00 for minors. At least some workers not covered by the national minimum wage rate of $1.60 per hour probably became covered by the state's new minimum wage. Workers covered by both state and national minimum wage rates automatically are eligible for the higher of the two. Subsequent laws passed at least every six years repeatedly raised Oregon's minimum wage. In the early 2000s, a new law tied increases in Oregon's minimum wage to increases in the U.S. consumer price index. Oregon's minimum was $7.95 an hour in 2008, fourth highest in the U.S. after Washington ($8.07), California ($8.00), and Massachusetts ($8.00).

A Shorter Workweek

What's the workweek like in Oregon? Workers in the nation's manufacturing sector typically work about forty hours per week and have done so at least since the mid-1900s. However, the overall average workweek in Oregon is substantially less. Because workers in service-based industries typically work fewer hours, the increase in service sector jobs caused average weekly hours for all workers to decline from more than thrity-eight in the mid-1960s to fewer than thirty-four in 2007.

Employees work the deli counter at Grande Foods in Cornelius, Oregon—photo taken by Todd Brown

STATESMAN JOURNAL —
JULY 18, 1995

Wage law to change figures

A new law allows Oregon's Bureau of Labor and Industries to administer statewide surveys for the purpose of determining prevailing wage rates. Previously, Oregon used the rates determined by the federal government. The new surveys will be funded by a small tax on the employers who perform prevailing wage work.

Eloise Ebert, Oregon state librarian from 1958–1976, photo taken in 1949—courtesy Oregon State Library

Women as a Percent of All People in Oregon Identified as Workers

Source: U.S. Census Bureau, decennial census data.

A further reason for the overall decline is that the average workweek for those service workers also fell, from more than thirty-seven hours in the mid-1960s to fewer than thirty-three hours by the late 1980s. The rise of part-time retail and hospitality jobs also contributed to this decline in average weekly hours: the average for retail trade fell from thirty-five hours in the early 1970s to thirty hours in 2007; the average for leisure and hospitality fell from more than thirty-two hours in the mid-1960s to about twenty-six hours in 2007.

Women in the Workplace

In the Oregon of 1960, only 40 percent of women between the ages of eighteen and sixty-four were in the labor force, and the share was even lower—about 32 percent—for women in the prime childbearing years of ages twenty-five to thirty-four. Meanwhile, almost 91 percent of men between the ages of eighteen and sixty-four were in the labor force. Of all employed adults in the 1960 census, 68 percent were men and 32 percent were women. These percentages changed substantially over the following forty-six years. In 2006, 54 percent of Oregon's employed adults were men and 46 percent were women.

While the overall numbers have changed quite a bit, those proportions are not always the case. Take secretarial work, for instance. As computers took over many clerical tasks formerly done by secretaries, it would seem logical that clerical positions would have declined between 1950 and today. Not so. Clerical workers (now called "office and administrative support") made up 13 percent of jobs in 1960 (and were 73 percent female), and they make up around 14 percent today (and are 75 percent female). Computers haven't replaced clerical workers so much as allowed them to work more efficiently.

Women increased their share of all U.S. sales jobs from 36 percent in 1960 to 49 percent in 2006. But more women also work as professional and technical workers (38 percent in 1960 vs. 57 percent today). For service jobs, the trend is reversed. In 1960, women dominated the service sector (63 percent). In 2006, that number had dropped (57 percent female). Throughout the past one hundred and fifty years, women in the paid labor force have tended to fill lower-paying jobs—due in no small part to factors like the inequality in pay between genders, the limited availability of higher-paying jobs, and the limited availability of job training. However, this tendency has declined since the mid-1900s, and today more women are graduating from college and filling top-level positions.

Organized Labor Today

During the first half of the twentieth century, unions were a force to be reckoned with as they used their collective bargaining power to gain rights and benefits from employers. Between 1945 and 1980, nationwide membership in labor unions increased, though it did not grow as fast as the workforce as a whole. Union membership stood at 14.3 million in 1945 and then peaked in 1978 at over 20 million.

Beginning in the 1960s, farm workers in Oregon, mainly of Hispanic background, began actively seeking better working and living conditions on Oregon farms. This coincided with the creation of the United Farm Workers Union by Cesar Chavez. Groups formed in Oregon to create better housing, healthcare, and education for migrant workers.

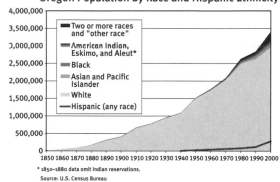

Oregon Population by Race and Hispanic Ethnicity

- Two or more races and "other race"
- American Indian, Eskimo, and Aleut*
- Black
- Asian and Pacific Islander
- White
- Hispanic (any race)

1850 1860 1870 1880 1890 1900 1910 1920 1930 1940 1950 1960 1970 1980 1990 2000

* 1850–1880 data omit Indian reservations.
Source: U.S. Census Bureau

Striking members of the Oregon Public Employees Union gather near the state capitol in Salem in 1995 — courtesy Oregon Employment Department

OREGON JOURNAL—MAY 3, 1975

Senate OKs Major Workmen's Comp Bill

The Oregon Senate passed a workmen's compensation bill that increased benefits payable from two-thirds of a worker's average weekly wages to 100 percent. The House, meanwhile, approved a measure that would, over several years, raise the taxable base for the unemployment insurance taxes paid by employers.

Between 1983 and 2007, however, union membership fell from about 22 percent of all workers in Oregon to only 14 percent. The general decline in union membership has led to fewer strikes and lockouts in the twenty-first century. However, unions still actively negotiate wages and benefits, and union members manage better than non-union workers when it comes to wages and benefits. Union members earn an average of $1.67 more per hour and are more likely to have employer-paid health care, pensions, and paid leave. A comprehensive list of unions shows thirty-one major unions in Oregon, representing such diverse occupations as government workers, bakers, postal workers, bricklayers, teachers, elevator constructors, painters, plumbers, steel workers, paper workers, and even television and radio reporters.

Minorities in the Workplace

Worker at a call center in Eugene handles inquiries from the public—photo taken by Tom Fuller

In addition to the influx of women, Oregon's workforce saw the introduction of many Hispanic and Asian workers during the second half of the twentieth century. While the Caucasian population doubled, going from 1.5 million in 1950 to 3 million in 2000, the minority population grew by a factor of almost fifteen, going from about 24,000 to 355,000. The state's Hispanic population—many of whom are counted as Caucasian—grew from just 1,500 to 275,000. This boosted the state's level of ethnic diversity and—for some jobs—added the requirement of being able to communicate in Spanish or Vietnamese in addition to English.

For thousands of years, Oregon has been a place of migration. From Native Americans who came here more than ten thousand years ago to the 1850s Oregon Trail migration, this state has attracted immigrants. Though many who traveled the Oregon Trail in the 1850s did so by wagon, another, more recent, group of immigrants came by boat, after escaping economic and political difficulties in a land very distant and very different from Oregon.

In the late 1970s and early 1980s, these refugees were spoken of in the press as "Vietnamese Boat People." Some of them made their homes, and found their livelihoods, in Oregon. Among them was Anna Ngo.

Worker assembles products at Patrick Industries in Woodburn—photo by Tom Fuller

Business Owner—Anna Ngo

Anna Ngo stood at the fence line of a neighbor's house looking off into the distance. The gentle smile on her face belied an inner turmoil that would change her life and the life of her family forever. It was 1981 in Vung Tau City, Vietnam. It might have appeared as if Anna was gazing contentedly at the bucolic landscape of her small hometown. In reality, she was afraid. In just seven weeks, Anna Ngo would set out on a perilous journey to find work, a home, and a new life in a place she had until then only dreamed about—America.

Anna became one of over a million Vietnamese to escape the prisons, re-education camps, and poverty that gripped her country after the Vietnam War. Prior to 1975, Anna's family owned a small store and traded in black pepper, coffee, and beans. Anna's father had been a famous cabinetmaker. All that changed when the government began taking land away, jobs became scarce, and the economy spiraled downward.

Anna knew her only chance was to break free of Vietnam. Her family sold nearly all their possessions to pay the $2,000.00 for a seat on a boat, one of thousands of boats that filled to well over capacity for the dangerous journey. In November of 1981 word came that the ship was ready. Anna said a tearful goodbye to her large family and got on board, not knowing if she would make it or ever see her family again.

The boat that carried her away from Vung Tau was only six feet wide and fifteen feet long. Seventy-four Vietnamese refugees crowded its decks so completely that there was no room for anyone to lie down. Vietnamese authorities arrived at the dock to stop the departure, so the crew left the food at the dock and took off. Anna spent five days and five sleepless nights aboard that boat with no food. "I almost died," she remembers.

Most passing ships ignored the little vessel bobbing about in rough seas. Finally, a fishing boat picked them up and deposited them in an Indonesian refugee camp. Anna spent twenty-seven months in that camp, sleeping on a piece of wood and wondering what had happened to her dreams of freedom. As she waited for someone in the United States to sponsor her, Anna spent time learning English during the day and at the library in the evenings. "No English, no job," she thought. When a camp official called her name one day, she knew her time had come—she was going to the United States.

Anna arrived at the Portland airport and was met by a cousin who had sponsored her into the United States. Because the cousin was not a part of Anna's immediate family, it had taken a long time to gain permission to bring Anna into the country. After taking some time to get acclimated, Anna attended Portland Community College, where she studied English and computers. Finally, in 1987, she obtained her first job, at Columbia Sportswear, sewing shirts. It

Anna Ngo stands at a neighbor's fence in 1984, seven weeks before leaving Vietnam—courtesy Anna Ngo

Anna Ngo (on the left) waits in an Indonesian refugee camp for sponsorship to the United States in 1984—courtesy Anna Ngo

2000s Average Cost of Consumer Goods
Apples, red, 1 lb $0.98
Bacon, sliced, 1 lb $3.78
Bananas, 1 lb $0.52
Bread, white, 1 lb $1.29
Butter, 1 lb $1.52
Cheese, cheddar, 1 lb $3.81
Coffee, ground, 1 lb $3.47
Eggs, AA, 1 dz $1.69
Flour, white, 1 lb $0.34
Ground beef, 1 lb $3.13
Milk, 1 gal $3.19
Oranges, navel, 1 lb $1.14
Sugar, white, 1 lb $0.55
Gasoline, unleaded, 1 gal $2.94
Toothpaste, 6 oz $3.05
Newspaper subscription, monthly $13.95
Movie, evening $9.60
Personal computer, desktop $550
New vehicle $28,400
iPod (120GB) $249

was a good job for someone with minimal English skills, Anna says. She had learned to sew in Vietnam, so it was a skill she already possessed. Her duties included laying out material on a pattern, cutting it into its proper shape, sewing the shirts together, putting buttons on them, and then packing them up for shipment. The job paid her $4.25 an hour (minimum wage) for a regular forty-hour workweek.

As her English improved, so did her job prospects. She left Columbia to assemble mainframe computers at Fujitsu Computers in Hillsboro. Her new position paid $6.75 an hour. She also got her driver's license and even carpooled to work.

Now established in the United States, Anna began thinking about what career she wanted to pursue. She went back to school part-time to learn cosmetology and worked at various salons, cutting and coloring hair.

Then in 1995 she took a giant step, opening her own salon, Family Salon, in Portland. But Anna didn't stop there. She wanted to help others train for jobs like she did, so in 2004 she purchased Anthony Beauty School where one hundred and fifty students attend each year.

Though the majority of students she trains are Vietnamese, she also has students who are Hispanic, Cambodian, Russian, and of European descent. No longer cutting hair herself, Anna spends her days overseeing three full-time instructors and a business manager. Working with her teachers, taking inventory, filling out paperwork, and making sure her graduates find jobs fills most of her ten- to fourteen-hour days, but it's well worth it: "Coming to the United States gave me a life so I could survive and provide for myself. And so I could help my family."

Anna married another Vietnamese boat person and now has a family of her own, but she sends money back to her family in Vietnam, takes care of expenses for numerous underprivileged Vietnamese young people, and plans to open up her own beauty school in her home county. Her aim is not to bring more refugees to the United States, but to help create jobs back home. "My life is here in the U.S., but my heart will always be in Vietnam."

Management

After many years of working in a career and honing their skills, some workers move into management or business ownership. In addition to the state's many owner-operators of unincorporated businesses, there were almost eighty-one thousand management-level jobs in Oregon in 2006. About one-quarter of these jobs were in general or operations management and were among the highest-paid jobs in the state, with annual wages averaging more than $100,000.00 in 2008. Managers formulate policies, manage daily operations, and plan the use of materials and human resources.

Manager, Kroger Company—Jim Aalberg

Jim Aalberg punches the buttons on his phone with purpose. He's trying to set up a conference call with London, and he has little patience for the system, which seems to want him to keep pressing the same buttons. "I already did that!" he says to no one in particular. Though he might seem demanding to some, when it comes to getting fair treatment for his company, nothing stands in Jim's way. His eyes flash behind square glasses as he pushes agents in London to get the best deal on re-insurance from Lloyd's of London and others for his company.

As Vice President for Corporate Insurance, Jim is responsible for the insurance coverage of buildings and employees in thirty-eight states—billions in assets. Managers like Jim make up just over 2 percent of Oregon's present workforce, supplying over twenty thousand jobs. His office, at Kroger subsidiary Fred Meyer, overlooks a beautiful courtyard in Southeast Portland. But Jim's focused on London, and making sure the "tower" of insurance he is constructing will be strong enough to withstand any assault.

Jim doesn't spend much time in his Portland office. Next week he's off to Ohio, to corporate HQ, and then on to Atlanta. On his desk sit thick files of insurance claims for flood damage to Midwest stores. Kroger owns the companies that insure these stores, but he goes over the claims with a fine tooth comb, making sure the stores get restocked and claims are paid quickly and fairly. Jim is a very pleasant person, but relishes pushing staff and insurance agents "to the wall," as he says, to get the most for every dollar he spends.

Jim didn't start his career as a corporate officer, of course. He started in the mailroom at the Bank of California—seventeen years old and just out of high school. In fact, he says he spent more time in the mailroom than most—almost four years. That was because he attended college at Portland State University in the mornings, then skipped lunch and reported for work right at noon.

STATESMAN JOURNAL—
APRIL 17, 2005

PERS costs will increase, report says

The Oregon Supreme Court ruled on the reforms made in 2003 by the Oregon legislature to the Public Employees Retirement System, deciding to keep some and overturn other changes. The ruling decreased the total amount of unfunded liability, but by less than the original legislation. Rates for employers are expected to increase substantially. Overall, all parties agree that the system is doing better because of the reforms.

Jim Aalberg begins his conference call in his Portland office in the Kroger Corporation Fred Meyer headquarters—photo taken by Tom Fuller

2000s Average Per Capita Consumer Spending Nationwide

Food
$2,753

Alcohol
$257

Housing—Shelter
$4,956

Housing—Utilities
$1,193

Housing—All Other
$1,567

Clothing
$818

Transportation
$3,906

Healthcare
$1,097

Entertainment
$1,142

Personal Care
$262

Reading
$55

Education
$365

Tobacco
$107

Miscellaneous
$404

Donations
$904

Insurance & Savings
$2,324

But working up from nothing was nothing new to Jim Aalberg. He credits his tenacity and work ethic to his great-great-great-grandfather, John West, who came to Oregon in 1850 to carve out a life on the Columbia River, near Astoria (read John West's story on page 52). Jim says of his ancestor:

> The thing that amazed me about John West, how could a man who was thirty-nine come out for the Gold Rush, leaving his family behind? His tenacity is an inspiration. If you think you have a tough commute down Highway 26—he had a two day commute to Portland to buy supplies.

John West built a sawmill by himself and then helped create an industry canning and shipping salmon around the world. That same entrepreneurial spirit fills Jim. The corporate philosophy at Kroger allows Jim to be creative and ask tough questions. That's actually why Jim works for Kroger. When Kroger acquired Fred Meyer in 1999, most of the Fred Meyer management left. Kroger asked Jim, then the treasurer of Fred Meyer, to stay on and oversee the transfer of the cash management systems to the new owner.

A funny thing happened, though. Jim did such a good job, and had such historical knowledge of Fred Meyer, that they offered him the position of treasurer for Kroger. As a sixth-generation Oregonian, a move from Oregon was not going to work for Jim. So Kroger let him stay in Portland to oversee their multi-million dollar insurance division. Having been a commercial banker before taking the job as Fred Meyer's treasurer, Jim didn't know anything about insurance. After a rough first year educating himself about insurance and questioning a lot of practices, Jim is pretty comfortable these days.

Today, the conversation on the phone is polite, but you can hear in his comments and the tone of his voice that Jim wants results and that a manager in Jim's employ who has recently made some wide-sweeping conclusions without thinking them through is going to hear about it later. When he stops to think about it, Jim says he owes a good deal of his success to John West, even when dealing in insurance. One example Jim uses goes back to 1882, when John West's store burned to the ground. An insurance company back then refused payment and John went to court to make them pay what was fair. Jim says he has inherited those qualities of insisting on equity and looking out for your own.

Volunteering as Work

Tom Burnett and Joanne Broadhurst

As this account of what work was like over Oregon's one hundred and fifty years of statehood nears its conclusion, we return to where it started—the home of Philip Foster (whose story is on page 58), in the fields near Eagle Creek. A century and a half after Philip helped get immigrants through those last miles to Oregon, Tom Burnett and Joanne Broadhurst help transport Oregonians of the twenty-first century back to the nineteenth.

At the beginning of this book, we left Tom chopping wood for the Philip Foster Farm store. About fifty yards away stands a new old-granary. Tom rebuilt the structure, which had first been put up near the turn of the twentieth century, using materials and methods similar to those of the original builder. Inside, it's quiet except for the clicking sound of a keyboard in use. Joanne hunches over her brand-new computer, typing entries into a piece of museum management software while surfing the Internet to research family history web sites. Tom and Joanne are brother and sister, and using methods both old and new, they guard a family history that forms a crucial part of the Oregon story.

Tom retired from his last job, a nineteen-year career as a corporate planner and marketer for Portland General Electric, in 1996. Far from spending his days on the golf course or traveling around the world, Tom works on the farm, traveling back in time one hundred and fifty years.

Tom and Joanne's great-great-grandfather Philip Foster came to Oregon and purchased a farm at Eagle Creek in 1847 (called Foster's originally, then Jackknife in 1890). Philip Foster contracted to build the Barlow Road, the last one-hundred-and-fifty-mile leg on the Oregon Trail, and built up his farm as sort of a destination resort with home-cooked meals, a blacksmith's shop, cabins for lodging, and a store.

Over the years, the family sold off parts of the property. Philip Foster's son, Gus Burnett, purchased back one hundred acres in 1903 (see Gus's story on page 92). Two acres of the original 640-acre land grant were donated to the local Jackknife-Zion-Horseheaven (JZH) Historical Society in 1992. This generosity provided Tom and Joanne (and many other volunteers) with a vision that will occupy the rest of their lives—the restoration of the Philip Foster Farm as a living history site.

OREGONIAN—AUGUST 1, 1965

Metal Pact Accepted in Portland; Vote May Turn Scales In Favor Of New Contract

Preliminary vote tallies show that the majority of the locally striking metal tradesmen union members favored a contract offered by the West Coast Shipbuilders' Association. Results would be announced after votes from all of the striking West Coast unions were totaled.

Tom Burnett repairs a gate post at the entrance to the Philip Foster Farm in Eagle Creek—photo taken by Tom Fuller

Tom Burnett and Joanne Broadhurst stand in front of an 1860s barn he has restored using period techniques and tools—photo taken by Tom Fuller

Tom currently oversees maintenance and construction on the five-acre farm, which is rated as one of the best historic sites in the state. The farm includes an 1860s barn, the 1883 Foster family farmhouse, a re-creation of Foster's store, heirloom flower and vegetable gardens, a historic apple orchard, and what is possibly the oldest lilac tree in Oregon.

But what really excites Tom Burnett is not simply refurbishing or re-creating the buildings on Philip Foster's farm, but doing it just as Philip himself would have. "I look back in history, like the re-creation of the lean-to on the barn. We had a picture of it. If you look at the barn today, it looks just like that picture. You can't tell that it's not original. The boards were out of a hundred-year-old barn I tore down."

Tom salvages lumber from any period buildings that are being torn down and goes through what are often hundred-year-old boards to find just the right ones to use restoring his grandfather's granary. When constructing buildings, Tom uses a mallet, chisel, and drill to make mortises (holes used to join two pieces of wood together), and uses crosscut saws for sizing beams rather than rely on modern conveniences like power saws.

I have to imagine "how did they do it?" They knew how to do stuff. I don't know how to do these things, but I can imagine and look and think 'How would they do it?' How would I do it involves how they must have done it. I'm trying to create the environment that he had. I will use very old material. I'll put boards up with bugs in them. It'll last another hundred years. I try not to use anything new except that which I have to. If I'm going to put a post in the ground, for instance, I have to put a pressure treated one in. I can't let the signs rot off and fall down in eight years! I try not to do things twice.

To put up a re creation of Foster's store, Tom and six other workers used a hand crane to lift the beams and rafters in place. Tom says Philip Foster would have had to make his own crane with horses providing the power. For the blacksmith shop, Tom spent six days cutting posts and beams to size, and then making the mortises and tenons (the small piece that goes into the mortise) to hold it together. When it came time to assemble it by hand, it took only twenty minutes.

Doing things the old-fashioned way brings Tom a great deal of satisfaction and connects him in a very real way with those in his family who settled this land. He explains:

> I get rewards out of this. I get rewards out of doing things that are not easy. I see people—the first thing they do is go get a machine to move some dirt. I'll go get the wheelbarrow and a shovel. That's why I'm sixty-eight and the slimmest I've been since I was thirty. It gives me real pleasure to re-create what I thought was there. Part of the reason is that people say, "this is a really neat place."

You can tell Tom gets a kick out of being able to do things the way Philip Foster or Gus Burnett (Tom's grandfather) did. It connects him to his family, and now he can connect that rich heritage to thousands of others who visit the once-again active Philip Foster Farm.

Though from the same family, Joanne Broadhurst is very different from her brother. While Tom is outside digging a post hole, she is inside digging through family historical records—organizing, cataloging, and preserving them for the future. A retired accounting teacher, CPA, and small business owner, Joanne feels well suited to her new job as curator for the JZH Historical Society museum: "Using technology fits the way I do things better. I can't look at something and build it like Tom. Being logical and detailed and putting things in their proper little boxes, that's me. I like the technology of doing that."

2000s Average Annual Income

Retail Salespersons
$26,767

Cashiers
$28,603

Bookkeeping, Accounting, and Auditing Clerks
$33,815

Registered Nurses
$68,990

Waiters and Waitresses
$21,327

General and Operations Managers
$102,716

Postsecondary Teachers
$76,381

Carpenters
$40,996

Computer Programmers
$69,447

Economists
$77,450

Automotive Mechanics
$38,514

WILLAMETTE WEEK—JULY 6, 2005

Mobile Espresso Business. Established and profitable. All equip is in excellent condition. Get licensed and have your own business! Includes training and marketing materials. Asking $42,000.

Joanne has a lot to put in order. The Fosters and Burnetts saved lots of paper. Records and letters were more valuable than furniture to them, because they created a record for future generations to learn about what the family did. Subsequently, they have detailed records on just what went into their great-grandmother Lucy Burnett's house, including furniture lists, plants, and wallpaper. It's a lot to go through, but what Joanne learns will allow them to create a near-perfect reproduction of an early turn-of-the-century Oregon house. Joanne tells a story of one of her documents:

> There was one letter from one of [grandpa] Gus's brothers: "Do not sell Papa's books." We have Papa's books in the house. I remember those books from when I was a child. People would cringe the way they were kept on a little shelf behind the stove. We had law books, medical books, dictionaries, all dated in the 1850s. They were educated people. Books were important, education was important.

They passed that emphasis on education down to their children and grandchildren. Most of Joanne's family attended college. She and Tom have advanced degrees. She taught high school accounting and business. Joanne says:

> Education and having books around was just part of how we grew up. They were just there. I never considered that I wasn't going to go to college. It was never discussed. And when the time came for me to go to college, and farming was not bringing in a lot of good money, my dad went back to work. He chose to do that so I could go to college.

Now Joanne educates others on the importance of history and helps families discover their roots. She gets a lot of visitors and phone calls to the Philip Foster Farm

The country store on the Philip Foster Farm—photo taken by Tom Fuller

from people asking for records about those who came down the Barlow Road. Recently, she worked on a small, four-tombstone cemetery in the area. She discovered a person's name and dates of birth and death. After searching the Internet, she discovered that the family had written that their ancestor had died in Kansas, but here was that ancestor, buried along with a mother and some sisters in Eagle Creek, Oregon. Joanne set the record straight.

Joanne plans to do this with many of the records she is cataloging at the farm—connect families and help them to find more information about their pasts. Right now, stacks of boxes line the granary, but soon Joanne the organizer will have them sorted, cataloged, and available.

And that's what the pioneer spirit means to Joanne—the desire to pass on the importance of something that existed at the beginning so you can see its progression. "I think we learn so much from the past that we can appreciate why things happen. We've been raised on good old-fashioned solid values—being honest, working hard, and the 'can do' attitude. I want to pass that on to my grandson."

The future holds exciting things for Joanne and Tom. In addition to maintenance on the buildings and cataloging historical records, they hope to begin restoring Lucy and Josiah Burnett's house across the street from the Philip Foster Farm. Used continuously as a private residence for one hundred and forty years, one day the house will give everyone an opportunity to step back in time to visit Oregon pioneers at home.

Conclusion

In many ways, work has changed greatly over the past one hundred and fifty years. Our typical working environments have shifted from farms and mines to logging camps and sawmills to office buildings and retail stores and high-tech factories. Most of us spend less working time outdoors than our ancestors did, and our jobs demand less physical exertion.

Amazing advancements in technology, nurtured by decades of scientific discoveries and abundant and inexpensive energy resources, now allow us to produce massive quantities of goods with less effort than any time in history. Modern technology, energy resources, and transportation infrastructure also allow us to deliver those goods very rapidly to more people spread out over long distances. Compare this to the effort and time spent in hauling wheat to market in a horse-drawn cart over rutted and sometimes muddy roads, as the founders of Oregon would have done.

Increased population and transportation allow for much more trade, which in turn allows us to specialize more in the type of work we do. Carpenters, for instance, no longer need to build their own doors; that's done by a door manufacturer employing workers who do nothing all day but build doors. Increased specialization typically involves operating sophisticated and expensive machines.

In many cases, it requires workers to possess a large body of knowledge and skills gained through many years of schooling or lengthy on-the-job training.

While early Oregon workers had to be somewhat self-sufficient, the rise of specialization has made us more interdependent. We rely on the products of specialized factories rather than learning all the skills and gathering all the tools and resources needed to be self-sufficient. For example, if the door factory closed, it would take the carpenter of today much more effort to build a door than a carpenter of 1850, because he or she would have to learn new skills and obtain unfamiliar tools.

With so much time and effort invested in a specialized field of work, modern workers tend to work in only one field for many years. In contrast, early Oregon settlers commonly engaged in two or more paying jobs throughout the year or from one year to the next, such as helping harvest wheat for a few weeks, then clearing land or driving cattle or surveying or logging or working on a railroad. Modern-day specialization not only supports a high level of productivity—the ability to produce more and higher-quality goods and services—but also brings greater fragility of employment. When workers lose their highly specialized jobs, they face uncertain prospects of finding new jobs that use their highly developed but narrow set of skills and that pay similar wages.

With few exceptions, we work in much bigger cities, and many of us in much larger organizations than were common fifty or one hundred years ago. Almost all of us come into contact with more people each day than our ancestors would have, either in person or through today's many telecommunications tools.

Minorities and people with disabilities face less discrimination than they used to, making our workplaces more diverse. Similarly, women are now far more common in the workforce than they used to be. As women became a part of the paid labor force, their manual labor around the house was at least partly automated or replaced with purchased goods and services. This provided demand for additional workers to make and sell new labor-saving machines, as well as many of the goods and services formerly produced at home.

Government plays a bigger role in regulating our work environment than in the earliest part of the twentieth century, though not as much as during some of the later decades. Although we may not take daily notice of most government regulations, they shape the limits of paid work young people can do, the length of our workweek and working day, the level of safety standards and accommodations for people with disabilities required of businesses, the access minorities have to desirable jobs, and even the minimum wage an employee can be paid. These regulations were absent or much less restrictive in Oregon's earliest years.

In many ways, jobs have changed dramatically over Oregon's one hundred and fifty years of statehood. But some things have not changed. Our drive to accomplish, the need to provide for our families, and the desire to live in this special place will likely keep us inventing new ways of working and will attract new people here, ensuring that Oregon is at work for many years to come.

Resources

The following materials were very helpful in developing this book and could provide you with more information on some of the topics covered.

A Peculiar Paradise, a History of Blacks In Oregon, 1788-1940, McLagan, Elizabeth, The Georgian Press, 1980.

A Rural Carpenter's World, Franklin, Wayne, University of Iowa Press, 1990.

America's Working Women, Baxandall, Rosalyn, W. W. Norton & Company, 1976.

Atlas of Oregon, 2nd ed., Loy, William G. (editor), Stuart Allen, Aileen R. Buckley, and James E. Meacham, University of Oregon Press, 2001.

Careers for People on the Move and Other Road Warriors, Eberts, Marjorie, McGraw-Hill Professional, 2001.

Crossing the Plains, Rickard, Aileen Barker, 1988.

Dreams of the West, Ooligan Press, 2007.

Nosotros, The Hispanic People of Oregon, Gamboa, Erasmo (editor), Oregon Council for the Humanities, 1995.

Oregon Teachers Remember, Borgman, Isabelle, compiler, Sudden Printing, 1976.

Pioneer Woolen Mills in Oregon, Lomax, Alfred L. Binford & Mort, 1941.

Schoolmarms, Rees, Helen Guyton, Binford & Mort, 1983.

Talking on Paper, An Anthology of Oregon Letters and Diaries, Applegate, Shannon & Terence O'Donnell, Oregon State University Press, 1994.

Tea at the Blue Lantern Inn, Whitaker, Jan, St. Martin's Press, 2002.

The American Northwest, A History of Oregon and Washington, Dodds, Gordon B., The Forum Press, Inc., 1986.

The Centennial History of Oregon, 1811-1912, Volume II, Gaston, Joseph, The S.J. Clark Publishing Company, 1912.

The Doctor in Oregon, A Medical History, Larsell, O., Oregon Historical Society, 1947.

The First Oregonians, Berg, Laura (editor), Oregon Council for the Humanities, 2007.

The Kalapuyans, Mackey, Harold, Mission Mill Museum Association, 2004.

The Sandal and the Cave, Cressman, Luther S, Oregon State University Press, 2005.

This Was Cattle Ranching, Yesterday and Today, Paul, Virginia, Superior Publishing Company, 1973.

This Was Wheat Farming, Brumfield, Kirby, Superior Publishing Co., 1968.

Up From Slavery, The Umpqua Trapper, Abdill, George, Douglas County Historical Society, 1971.

Valley of the Rogues, Booth, Percy, Josephine County Historical Society, 1970.

William Emsley Jackson's Diary of a Cattle Drive From La Grande, Oregon to Cheyenne, Wyoming, in 1876, Jackson, William E., Ye Galleon Press, 1983.

Winning With People: The First 40 Years of Tektronix, Lee, Marshall, Tektronix, 1986.

With Her Own Wings, Smith, Helen Krebs (editor), Beattie & Company, 1948.

Yoncalla, Home of the Eagles, Kruse, Anne Applegate, 1950.

Index

Note: page numbers in *italics* indicate photographs.

Ooligan Press

Ooligan Press is a general trade press at Portland State University. In addition to publishing books that honor cultural and natural diversity, it is dedicated to teaching the art and craft of publishing.

As a teaching press, Ooligan makes as little distinction as possible between the press and the classroom. Under the direction of professional faculty and staff, the work of the Press is done by students enrolled in the Book Publishing graduate program at PSU. Publishing profitable books in real markets provides projects in which students combine theory with practice.

Ooligan Press offers the school and general community a full range of publishing services, from consulting and planning to design and production. Ooligan Press students, having already received important "real world" training while at the university and in various internship positions in the greater Portland area, are ideal candidates for jobs in the country's growing community of independent publishers.

This edition of *Oregon at Work: 1859–2009* was produced by the following students on behalf of Ooligan Press:

Acquisitions Editors
Kylin Larsson
Megan Wellman

Editors
Scott Parker
Leah Sims
Ian VanWyhe
Mel Wells

Cover & Interior Designer
Kelley R. Dodd

Proofreaders
Daniel Chabon
Amanda Johnson
Matt Schrunk
Mel Wells

Marketing
Natalie Emery
Whitney Quon
Carole Studebaker
Ooligan Press
   Marketing Workgroup